GRAMMAR
101

Level 3

Grammar 101 Level 3

지은이 넥서스영어교육연구소
펴낸이 임상진
펴낸곳 (주)넥서스

출판신고 1992년 4월 3일 제311-2002-2호 2-1
10880 경기도 파주시 지목로 5
Tel (02)330-5500 Fax (02)330-5555

ISBN 979-11-6165-137-8 54740
     979-11-6165-142-2 (SET)

www.nexusbook.com

※본 책은 워크북을 추가하고, After School Grammar의 콘텐츠를 재구성한 것입니다.

한번에 끝내는
중등 영문법

GRAMMAR

101

넥서스영어교육연구소 지음

Level 3

NEXUS Edu

GRAMMAR
101 is...

basic
'기초 과정의, 입문의, 기본의'라는 뜻의 Grammar 101 [wʌnouwʌ́n]으로
영문법 기초를 최단 기간에 마스터할 수 있도록 구성하였습니다.

easy
예비 중부터 누구나 쉽게 단계별로 공부할 수 있습니다.
Level 1~3까지는 중학교 과정을 쉽게 마스터할 수 있도록 구성되어 있습니다.

rich
각 Lesson의 Practice뿐만 아니라 워크북에서도 내신에 자주 등장하는
다양하고 풍부한 단답형, 서술형 문제를 제공합니다.

useful
문법뿐만 아니라 실용적인 다양한 표현을 배웁니다.
실생활에서 사용할 수 있는 실용적인 표현들을 엄선하여 예문에 활용했습니다.

systematic
체계적으로 공부할 수 있도록 구성하였습니다.
시험에 나올 수 있는 문제들을 체계적이고 반복적으로 학습하면서
문법의 원리와 규칙들을 자연스럽게 습득합니다.

confident
내신시험에 자신감을 심어줍니다.
문법을 알기 쉽게 설명하고 있으며, 각 학년에서 다루는 문법만을
집중적으로 공부함으로써 내신시험에 보다 효과적으로대비할 수 있습니다.

up to date
최신 기출문제 유형을 제공합니다.
전국 중학교에서 출제된 문법문제들을 각 학년별로 분석하여,
최신 문제 유형을 미리 학습할 수 있으며,
서술형 문제를 더욱 보충하여 내신시험에 대비할 수 있도록 했습니다.

1 Grammar Lesson

중요 핵심 문법을 빠르게 이해하고, 기억하기
쉽도록 도표, 도식, 그림을 이용하였습니다.
내신에 꼭 필요한 사항만을 담아, 최단기간에
각 단계별 영문법을 마스터할 수 있도록 구성
하였습니다.

2 Practice

다양한 유형의 풍부한 문제 풀이를 통해 내신
대비는 물론, 영어의 4가지 영역(L, R, S, W)
을 공부하는 기초를 습득할 수 있습니다. 문제
를 풀면서 자신의 취약점을 확인하고, 단계별
문제를 통해 기초부터 심화까지 학습할 수 있
습니다.

3 VOCA in Grammar

문법 문제 속에 있는 어휘를 찾아 앞에서 배운
기초 문법을 한 번 더 쉽게 확인할 수 있습니
다. 어휘의 영영풀이를 통해 어휘의 개념뿐만
아니라 문법의 기초 개념까지도 파악할 수 있
도록 구성하였습니다.

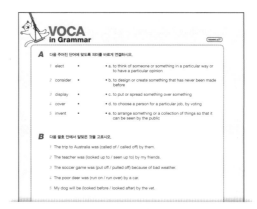

4 Workbook

각 레슨별로 최신 기출 문제 유형을 담아 다양한 문제풀이를 할 수 있도록 구성하였습니다. 각 Lesson 및 Practice 학습 후, 자기주도학습으로 워크북을 활용할 수 있도록 구성하였습니다.

5 Chapter Review

철저한 내신 분석을 통해 기출과 유사한 시험문제를 풀어볼 수 있도록 시험지 형태로 구성하였습니다. 챕터 안에서 배웠던 문법 사항들을 통합하여 학습할 수 있도록 하였습니다.

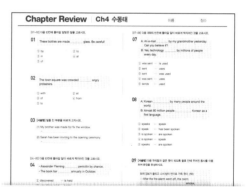

추가 제공 자료 (www.nexusbook.com)

어휘 리스트 & 테스트지

통문장 영작 테스트지

통문장 해석 테스트지

동사 · 비교급 변화표 & 테스트지

문법 용어집

모바일단어장 추가 제공

이 책의 차례

CONTENTS

Chapter

01

부정사

Grammar
Lesson 1

★ 명사적 역할 '~하기', '~하는 것' 등으로 해석

❶ 주어, 보어, 목적어 역할

주어	To drink enough water is good for your health. 물을 충분히 마시는 것이 건강에 좋다. → It is good for your health to drink enough water. (진주어)
보어	My dream is to be a scientist. 내 꿈은 과학자가 되는 것이다.
목적어	I planned to travel to Australia. 나는 호주로 여행을 계획했다.

❷ 의문사+to부정사

He didn't know what to do next. 그는 다음에 무엇을 해야 할지 몰랐다.

→ He didn't know what he should do next.

* 「의문사+ to부정사」는 문장에서 명사적 역할을 하며, 「의문사+주어+should+동사」로 바꿔 쓸 수 있다.

★ 형용사적 역할

❶ 명사 수식

It's time to leave for the airport. 공항으로 떠나야 할 시간이다.

❷ 「be+to부정사」 의무, 예정, 운명, 조건 등

We are to finish our homework by 5 p.m. (의무) 우리는 오후 다섯 시까지 숙제를 끝내야 한다.

The public library is to open next Monday. (예정) 공공도서관은 다음 월요일에 개관할 예정이다.

❸ 「to부정사+전치사」

John needed a true friend to talk with. (to talk with a true friend) John은 이야기를 나눌 진정한 친구가 필요했다.

They want a small, cozy house to live in. (to live in a small, cozy house) 그들은 거주할 작고 아늑한 집을 원한다.

★ 부사적 역할

목적 ~하기 위해	The kids went to the aquarium to see the dolphin show. = The kids went to the aquarium in order to [so as to] see the dolphin show. 아이들은 돌고래 쇼를 보기 위해 수족관에 갔다.
판단의 근거 ~하다니	He must be kind to help his mother. 어머니를 돕는 걸 보니 그는 친절함에 틀림없다.
감정의 원인 ~해서	She was excited to pass the exam. 그녀는 시험에 통과해서 신이 났었다.
결과 ~해서 그 결과로 ...하다	The girl grew up to be a doctor. 그 소녀는 자라서 의사가 되었다.
형용사 수식 ~하기에	This map is difficult to understand. 이 지도는 이해하기 어렵다.

Practice

Answers p.02

A 다음 두 문장이 같은 뜻이 되도록 문장을 완성하시오.

1 To travel in the wintertime is harsh.

→ _____ is harsh _____.

2 To talk loudly on the train is impolite.

→ _____ is impolite _____.

3 To run on the escalator is dangerous.

→ _____ is dangerous _____.

B 다음 〈보기〉에서 알맞은 것을 골라 대화를 완성하시오.

> **Hint**
> what to do 무엇을 해야 할지
> how to do 어떻게 해야 할지
> where to go 어디를 가야 할지
> when to do 언제 해야 할지
> whether to do 해야 할지 말지
> which to do 어느 것을 해야 할지

보기 where to go   how to use   what to wear

1 A: Are you ready to go? It's time to leave for the party.

B: No, I don't know _____! I don't like any of my clothes.

2 A: Have you decided _____ for summer vacation?

B: Sure. My sister and I will go to Switzerland for mountain climbing.

3 A: Hey, Robert. Could you help me to copy this document?

B: I'm sorry. This copy machine is new. I don't know _____ it.

C 다음 〈보기〉에서 동사를 골라 알맞은 형태로 바꿔 문장을 완성하시오.

> **Plus**
> 「to부정사+전치사」
> 전치사가 필요한지 아닌지는 목적어를
> to부정사 뒤에 놓아보면 쉽게 알 수 있다.
> I need a pen to write with.
> (O) to write with a pen
> (X) to write a pen

보기 ask   write   receive   watch   talk   visit

1 He went to the U.S.A. _____ his niece.

2 Molly needed a piece of paper _____ on.

3 He wanted _____ her a question about her childhood.

4 I was very happy _____ the musical with you today.

5 She is the first person _____ a scholarship in her family.

6 I have worries and problems _____ about.

Eng-Eng VOCA

harsh	cruel, severe and unkind
impolite	rude, not polite
copy machine	a machine that makes paper copies of documents
childhood	the period of someone's life when they are a child
scholarship	an amount of money given to someone to help pay for their education

Grammar
Lesson 2

★ to부정사의 의미상의 주어 to부정사의 행위자

	일반인	It is good to go to bed early and get enough sleep. 일찍 자고, 충분한 수면을 취하는 것이 좋다.
	주어와 동일	We like to listen to rock music. 우리는 록음악 듣는 것을 좋아한다.
	목적어와 동일	He wanted <u>me</u> to go with him. 그는 내가 자기와 함께 가기를 원했다.
행위자가 따로 존재	형용사 「for+목적격」	It was impossible for him to get to the meeting on time. 그가 회의 시간에 맞춰 도착하는 것은 불가능했다.
	사람의 성격을 나타내는 형용사 「of+목적격」	It was very kind of her to volunteer to help flood victims. 그녀는 친절하게도 홍수 피해자를 자청해서 도와주었다.

★ to부정사의 시제

동일 시제 「to+동사원형」	Tom <u>seems</u> to be very excited. Tom은 매우 신이 나 보인다. → It <u>seems</u> that Tom is very excited. Tom <u>seemed</u> to be very excited. Tom은 매우 신이 나 보였다. → It <u>seemed</u> that Tom was very excited.
앞선 시제 「to+have+p.p.」	She <u>seems</u> to have forgotten my name. 그녀는 내 이름을 잊어버린 것처럼 보인다. → It <u>seems</u> that she forgot my name. She <u>seemed</u> to have forgotten my name. 그녀는 내 이름을 잊어버린 것처럼 보였다. → It <u>seemed</u> that she had forgotten my name.

* 동사의 시제와 부정사의 시제가 같으면 「to+동사원형」을, 동사의 시제보다 부정사의 시제가 앞설 경우 「to+have+p.p.」를 쓴다.

★ to부정사의 태

능동 「to+동사원형」	The students wanted to paint their classroom in green. 학생들은 교실을 녹색으로 칠하기를 원했다.
수동 「to+be+p.p.」	The students wanted <u>their classroom</u> to be painted in green. 학생들은 교실이 녹색으로 칠해지기를 원했다.

Practice

Answers p.02

A 다음 빈칸에 for와 of 중 알맞은 것을 넣어 문장을 완성하시오.

Hint

of+목적격:
주로 사람을 칭찬하거나 비판할 때 씀
(kind, nice, good, careless, clever, wise, polite, generous, foolish, stupid, rude, silly 등)

1 It was careless _____ him to drive that fast.

2 It is dangerous _____ you to go out late at night.

3 It is very kind _____ her to share her room with us.

4 It was foolish _____ Adam to spend all his money on shoes.

5 It is too difficult _____ you to solve the problem.

B 다음 두 문장이 같은 뜻이 되도록 문장을 완성하시오.

1 Janice seemed to like playing soccer.

→ It seemed that Janice _____ playing soccer.

2 It seems that she talked on the phone for quite a long time.

→ She seems _____ on the phone for quite a long time.

3 It seemed that he was worried about his English test.

→ He seemed _____ worried about his English test.

4 Brian seems to have been very upset about his parents' decision.

→ It seems that Brian _____ very upset about his parents' decision.

C 다음 주어진 단어의 알맞은 형태를 써서 문장을 완성하시오.

Hint

help+목적어+(to)+동사원형

1 My old socks need _____. (mend)

2 She promised to help me _____ an essay. (write)

3 Everyone wants _____ by other people. (understand)

4 We don't have _____ the homework by today. (complete)

5 He didn't expect _____ to the housewarming party. (invite)

Eng-Eng VOCA

careless	not giving enough attention to what you are doing
share	to have or use something with others
quite	very, but not extremely
essay	a piece of writing that tells a person's opinions about a subject
complete	to finish doing something

Grammar
Lesson 3

❶ to부정사를 목적어로 취하는 동사

> afford, agree, ask, choose, decide, expect, hope, learn, manage, need, offer,
> plan, promise, refuse, seem, want, wish ...

I can't afford to go on vacation this year. 나는 올해는 휴가를 갈 여유가 없다.

My sister and I planned to ride a bike along the river this evening.
내 여동생과 나는 오늘 저녁에 강을 따라 자전거를 타기로 계획을 세웠다.

❷ 동명사를 목적어로 취하는 동사

> avoid, admit, consider, delay, deny, discuss, enjoy, finish, give up,
> go on, imagine, keep (on), mind, postpone, quit, suggest ...

Harry admitted cheating on the test. Harry는 시험에서 부정행위를 했다는 것을 인정했다.

Sally enjoys living in the countryside. Sally는 전원생활을 즐긴다.

❸ to부정사와 동명사를 모두 목적어로 취하며 뜻이 달라지지 않는 동사

> like, continue, begin, start, love ...

I like eating[to eat] chocolate ice cream. 나는 초콜릿 아이스크림 먹는 것을 좋아한다.

The sky was getting darker, and it started raining[to rain]. 하늘은 점점 더 어두워졌고 비가 내리기 시작했다.

❹ to부정사와 동명사를 모두 목적어로 취하지만, 뜻이 달라지는 동사

remember+to부정사 ~할 것을 기억하다	I'll remember to e-mail Brian, so don't worry. 내가 Brian에게 이메일 보낼 것을 기억할 테니까 걱정 마.
remember+동명사 ~했던 것을 기억하다	I remember e-mailing Brian this morning. 나는 오늘 아침에 Brian에게 이메일 보낸 것을 기억한다.
forget+to부정사 ~할 것을 잊다	I forgot to lock the bicycle, and now it's gone. 내가 자전거에 자물쇠를 거는 것을 잊어버려서 지금 그 자전거가 없어져 버렸다.
forget+동명사 ~했던 것을 잊다	I forgot leaving my cell phone at home, and I was looking for it all day. 나는 휴대 전화를 집에 두고 온 것을 잊고 온종일 그것을 찾았다.
regret+to부정사 ~하게 되어 유감이다	We regret to inform you that you have not been accepted. 당신이 받아들여지지 않았음을 알리게 되어 유감입니다.
regret+동명사 ~한 것을 후회하다	She didn't regret moving to Seoul. 그녀는 서울로 이사한 것을 후회하지 않았다.

Practice

Answers p.02

A 다음 주어진 동사를 알맞은 형태로 바꿔 문장을 완성하시오.

1 I want _____ my Christmas presents. (see)

2 Chris hopes _____ a brand-new sports car. (buy)

3 Can you imagine _____ without music? (live)

4 He decided _____ in Prague for two more weeks. (stay)

5 Kelly doesn't mind _____ her toys with her sister. (share)

6 Michael finished _____ the dishes before watching the news. (do)

B 다음 괄호 안에서 알맞은 것을 <u>모두</u> 고르시오.

1 I'm considering (to study / studying) abroad.

2 He managed (to get / getting) to the airport in time.

3 She promised (to buy / buying) David a laptop computer.

4 I started (to learn / learning) Spanish, but it is too difficult.

5 Tanya is afraid of water, and she doesn't like (to swim / swimming).

6 They gave up (to complain / complaining) about the noise from upstairs.

C 다음 우리말과 같은 뜻이 되도록 주어진 동사를 이용하여 문장을 완성하시오.

1 나는 상자를 움직여보려고 노력했지만, 움직이지 못했다. (move)

  → I tried _____ the box, but I couldn't.

2 그는 책상 위에 열쇠를 올려놓은 것을 기억했다. (put)

  → He remembered _____ the key on the desk.

3 그녀는 공항에 가기 전에 여권을 확인하는 것을 깜빡 잊어버렸다. (check)

  → She forgot _____ her passport before going to the airport.

4 나는 집에 가는 길에 우유를 사야 한다는 것을 기억했다. (buy)

  → I remembered _____ some milk on my way home.

5 당신이 시험에 합격하지 못했음을 알리게 되어 유감입니다. (inform)

  → We regret _____ you that you didn't pass the exam.

> **Hint**
>
> 「try+to부정사」
> ~을 하려고 애쓰다, 노력하다
> I tried to contact you all day,
> but you didn't answer.
> 나는 온종일 너에게 연락하려고 했지
> 만, 너는 받지 않았다.
>
> 「try+동명사」
> ~을 시도하다, (시험 삼아) 해보다
> Why don't you try turning
> the volume up?
> 소리를 좀 키워보는 게 어때?

Eng-Eng VOCA

brand-new	completely new
imagine	to form a picture in your mind of what someone/something might be like
consider	to think about something carefully in order to make a decision
manage	to succeed in doing something difficult
complain	to say that you are annoyed, not satisfied, or unhappy about something or someone

Grammar
Lesson 4

모바일단어장

★ 목적격보어로 쓰이는 to부정사, 원형부정사

❶ 목적격보어로 to부정사를 취하는 동사

「주어＋동사＋목적어＋to부정사」
allow, advise, ask, expect, tell, want, warn ...
My parents didn't <u>allow</u> me to go to the party. 우리 부모님은 내가 파티에 가는 것을 허락하지 않았다.
Her mother <u>told</u> her to send a package to her aunt in the U.S.A. 그녀의 어머니가 그녀에게 미국에 계신 이모님께 소포를 보내라고 했다.

❷ 목적격보어로 동사원형을 취하는 동사

「주어＋지각동사/사역동사＋목적어＋동사원형」
hear, smell, see, let, have, make
I <u>saw</u> Brenda play the flute. 나는 Brenda가 플루트 연주를 하는 것을 보았다.
My mother always <u>makes</u> me organize my desk before going to bed. 우리 어머니는 나에게 잠자기 전에 항상 책상을 정리하도록 시키셨다.

* help는 원형부정사와 to부정사를 모두 목적격보어로 취한다.

★ 관용 표현

enough＋명사＋to부정사 ～하기에 충분한 …	John saved <u>enough money</u> to buy new sneakers. John은 새 운동화를 사기에 충분한 돈을 저축했다.
형/부＋enough＋to부정사 ＝so＋형/부＋that＋주어＋can ～하기에 충분히 …하다, 매우 ～해서 ～할 수 있다	The water is <u>warm</u> enough (for us) to swim in all year round. → The water is so <u>warm</u> that <u>we</u> can <u>swim</u> in it all year round. 그 물은 매우 따뜻해서 일 년 내내 수영을 할 수 있다.
too＋형/부＋to부정사 ＝so＋형/부＋that＋주어＋can't ～하기에 너무 …하다, 너무 ～해서 …할 수 없다	Tim's sister is too <u>young</u> to bungee jump. → Tim's sister is so <u>young</u> that <u>she</u> can't bungee jump. Tim의 여동생은 너무 어려서 번지 점프를 할 수 없다.
to make matters worse 설상가상으로	I felt very cold. To make matters worse, it started to rain. 나는 너무 추웠다. 설상가상으로 비까지 내리기 시작했다.
to be honest (with you) ＝ to be frank (with you) ＝ to tell the truth 솔직히 말해서	I don't like math. To tell the truth, I'm really bad at calculating. 나는 수학을 좋아하지 않는다. 솔직히 말하면, 나는 계산을 정말 못한다.
be about to부정사 막 ～하려 하다	He was so tired that he was about to fall asleep. 그는 너무 피곤해서 곧 잠이 들려 하고 있었다.
be supposed to부정사 ～하기로 되어 있다, ～할 의무가 있다	She is supposed to give a presentation today. 그녀가 오늘 발표를 하기로 되어 있다.

Practice

Answers p.03

A 다음 괄호 안에서 알맞은 것을 고르시오.

1 I let my sister (use / to use) my laptop computer.

2 They saw Terry (leave / to leave) the classroom.

3 Edward advised her (take / to take) a train not a bus.

4 My doctor warned me not (exercise / to exercise) too much.

5 We hear our neighbor (play / to play) the piano every night.

6 My mother made my brother (pick / to pick) me up from school.

B 다음 괄호 안의 표현을 이용하여 주어진 문장과 같은 뜻이 되도록 문장을 완성하시오.

1 I can't do my homework. I'm too tired.

→ (too ~ to) _____

→ (so ~ that ~ can't) _____

2 He was too shy. He couldn't talk to me.

→ (too ~ to) _____

→ (so ~ that ~ can't) _____

3 She can't meet you for lunch. She's too busy.

→ (too ~ to) _____

→ (so ~ that ~ can't) _____

C 다음 우리말과 같은 뜻이 되도록 주어진 단어를 이용하여 문장을 완성하시오.

1 네가 전화를 걸었을 때 나는 집을 막 나서고 있었다. (leave, about)

→ I _____ the house when you called me.

2 내 남동생은 초등학교에 갈 만큼 충분히 나이가 들었다. (go, old)

→ My brother is _____ to elementary school.

3 그는 회의에 늦었다. 설상가상으로 길도 잃어버렸다. (make, matters)

→ He was late for the meeting. _____, he got lost.

4 그의 연기는 별로 좋지 않았다. 솔직히 말해서, 그의 연기는 끔찍했다. (be, honest)

→ His performance wasn't very good. _____, it was terrible.

Eng-Eng VOCA

advise	to tell someone what they should do
warn	to tell someone about possible danger or trouble
pick up	to let someone get into your car and take them somewhere
be about to	to be going to do something very soon
performance	the way an actor performs a part in a play or movie

VOCA
in Grammar

Answers p.03

A 다음 주어진 단어에 맞도록 의미를 바르게 연결하시오.

1 seem •　　　　　　• a. to think that something will happen

2 allow •　　　　　　• b. to feel sad or disappointed over something

3 deny •　　　　　　• c. to let someone have or do something

4 expect •　　　　　　• d. to appear to the mind or eye

5 regret •　　　　　　• e. to say that something is not true

B 다음 괄호 안에서 알맞은 것을 고르시오.

1 He (enjoys / promises) living in the countryside.

2 I am (managing / considering) studying abroad.

3 My doctor (warned / had) me not to exercise too much.

4 Edward (advised / suggested) her to take a train, not a bus.

5 John needed a true friend to (tell / talk) with.

C 다음 〈보기〉에서 알맞은 단어를 골라 문장을 완성하시오.

보기	tell	make	are	afford	hear

1 To _____ matters worse, it started to rain.

2 We _____ our neighbor play the piano every night.

3 I can't _____ to go on vacation this year.

4 To _____ the truth, I'm really bad at calculating.

5 We _____ to finish our homework by 5 p.m.

Chapter 02

분사와 분사구문

Grammar
Lesson 1

★ 분사의 종류

❶ 현재분사(동사원형+-ing) vs. 과거분사(동사원형+-ed/p.p.)

a <u>falling</u> <u>leaf</u> (능동) 떨어지는 나뭇잎　　　**fallen leaves** (수동) 떨어진 나뭇잎들(낙엽)
　　　명사 수식　　　　　　　　　　　　　　　　　명사 수식

a <u>sleeping</u> <u>baby</u> (능동) 잠자는 아기　　　a <u>wounded</u> <u>cat</u> (수동) 상처 입은 고양이

❷ 감정 분사　감정을 일으키는 원인이 되면 현재분사, 감정을 느끼게 되면 과거분사

The <u>news of his accident</u> was shocking to his friends.　그의 사고 소식은 그의 친구들에게 충격적이었다.

The <u>kids</u> were delighted to see the dinosaur exhibition.　아이들은 공룡 전시회를 보게 되어 기뻤다.

★ 분사의 쓰임

❶ 명사 수식　단독으로 쓰인 분사는 명사 앞에서, 수식어와 함께 쓰인 분사는 명사 뒤에서 명사를 수식한다.

It was an <u>exciting</u> <u>experience</u> to travel to the Amazon.　아마존 여행은 흥미진진한 경험이었다.

The <u>man</u> sitting next to Gary wants to see you.　Gary 옆에 앉아 있는 남자가 당신을 만나기를 원해요.

❷ 보어 역할　주어와 목적어를 보충 설명해주며 능동이면 현재분사가, 수동이면 과거분사가 목적격보어로 쓰인다.

The <u>audience</u> was completely impressed. (주격보어)　관객은 완전히 감동을 받았다.

The <u>English class</u> was very interesting. (주격보어)　영어수업은 아주 재미있었다.

We watched <u>Ken</u> baking Jin's birthday cake. (목적격보어)　우리는 Ken이 Jin의 생일 케이크를 굽는 것을 지켜보았다.

I found <u>my bicycle</u> hidden in the bushes. (목적격보어)　나는 풀숲에 숨겨져 있는 내 자전거를 발견했다.

★ 현재분사와 동명사의 구별

	현재분사	동명사
-ing+명사	a sleeping puppy 잠자는 강아지 (-ing가 명사의 행동을 설명: 강아지가 잠을 잠)	a sleeping bag 침낭 (-ing가 명사의 용도를 설명: 잠자기 위한 가방)
주어	-	Dancing makes me happy. 춤을 추는 것은 나를 행복하게 한다.
목적어	-	I like singing and dancing. 나는 노래하고 춤추는 것을 좋아한다.
목적격보어	I saw a boy dancing. 나는 한 소년이 춤을 추는 것을 보았다.	-
be -ing	He was teaching English. (진행시제) 그는 영어를 가르치고 있었다.	His job is teaching English. (주격보어: His job = teaching English) 그의 직업은 영어를 가르치는 것이다.

Practice

Answers p.03

A 다음 〈보기〉에서 알맞은 것을 골라 현재분사 또는 과거분사로 바꿔 문장을 완성하시오.

> **보기**   break   irritate   depress   glitter

1 A rainy day makes me _____.

2 We saw _____ stars in the dark sky.

3 I found the _____ cup on the dining table.

4 He kept asking me the same question, so I was _____.

현재분사	
형태	V-ing
의미	능동, 진행
쓰임	They watched Tim playing soccer. 그들은 Tim이 축구하는 것을 보았다. The dog was taking a nap. 강아지가 낮잠을 자고 있다.

과거분사	
형태	V-ed(p.p.)
의미	수동, 완료
쓰임	I wasn't invited to the party. 나는 그 파티에 초대되지 않았다. Have you heard from him lately? 최근에 그에게서 소식을 들은 적이 있니?

B 다음 〈보기〉와 같이 문장을 완성하시오.

> **보기** Her great efforts inspired the rest of the team members.
> → Her great efforts were ____inspiring____.
> → The rest of the team members were ____inspired____.

1 The hard work exhausted Ian.

→ Ian was _____ by the hard work.

→ The hard work was _____.

2 My test result disappointed my homeroom teacher.

→ My test result was _____.

→ My homeroom teacher was _____.

3 The big dog barking loudly frightened my little sister.

→ The big dog barking loudly was _____.

→ My little sister was _____ by the big dog barking loudly.

C 다음 밑줄 친 부분을 바르게 고쳐 쓰시오.

1 James likes <u>read</u> both novels and comic books.

2 You can try on clothes in the <u>fit</u> room.

3 The boy <u>stand</u> over there is my brother.

4 My grandfather is <u>fish</u> in the river now.

Eng-Eng VOCA

glitter	to shine brightly with little flashes of light
effort	work done by the mind or body
inspire	to make someone want to do something
exhaust	to use all of someone's mental or physical energy
frighten	to make someone suddenly feel afraid

Grammar
Lesson 2

★ 분사구문

❶ 분사구문 만들기

When I walked down the street, I ran into my English teacher.
　　① 　② 　　③

→ **Walking** down the street, I ran into my English teacher. 나는 길을 걷다가 우연히 영어 선생님을 만났다.

　① 부사절의 접속사 생략
　② 부사절의 주어와 주절의 주어가 같으면 부사절의 주어 생략
　③ 부사절의 동사를 -ing 형태로 바꾼다.

* 분사구문은 부사절의 접속사와 주어를 생략하고, 분사를 이용한 부사구로 바꾼 것이다.

❷ 의미

시간 ~때, ~동안, ~전에, ~후에	When we traveled in London, we watched a few musicals. → Traveling in London, we watched a few musicals. 우리는 런던을 여행했을 때 뮤지컬을 몇 편 보았다.
이유 ~ 때문에	Because he was tired, he went to bed early. → Being tired, he went to bed early. 그는 피곤해서 일찍 잠자리에 들었다.
조건 ~라면	If you leave right now, you won't miss the train. → Leaving right now, you won't miss the train. 네가 지금 바로 떠난다면, 기차를 놓치지 않을 거야.
양보 ~임에도 불구하고	Even though I had a cold, I went to the gym to exercise. → Having a cold, I went to the gym to exercise. 나는 감기에 걸렸지만, 운동을 하러 체육관에 갔다.
부대상황 (동시동작, 연속동작) ~하면서	While he was having dinner, Tom watched TV. → Having dinner, Tom watched TV. Tom은 저녁을 먹으면서 TV를 봤다. All the audience stood up and then danced to the music. → All the audience stood up, dancing to the music. 모든 청중들이 일어나서 춤을 췄다.

❸ 「접속사+분사구문」

While he was attending college, Peter worked as a fashion model. Peter는 대학에 다니는 동안 패션모델로 일했다.

→ While attending college, Peter worked as a fashion model.

* 분사구문의 뜻을 명확히 하기 위해 접속사를 남겨두기도 한다.

Practice

Answers p.04

A 다음 〈보기〉와 같이 부사절을 분사구문으로 바꿔 문장을 완성하시오.

Hint
부사절을 이끄는 접속사

시간	when, while, as, after, before
이유	because, as, since
조건 양보	if, unless, even if, although, though, even though

보기 When I ran to the classroom, I slid down the hallway.
→＿＿＿＿Running to the classroom, I slid down the hallway.＿＿＿＿

1 If you study hard, you'll pass the exam.
→ ＿＿＿＿＿＿＿＿＿＿＿＿＿＿＿＿＿＿＿＿＿＿＿＿＿＿

2 Even though she was sick, she went to school.
→ ＿＿＿＿＿＿＿＿＿＿＿＿＿＿＿＿＿＿＿＿＿＿＿＿＿＿

3 Because he wanted to buy a computer, he got a part-time job.
→ ＿＿＿＿＿＿＿＿＿＿＿＿＿＿＿＿＿＿＿＿＿＿＿＿＿＿

4 While I was waiting for my sister, I read a newspaper.
→ ＿＿＿＿＿＿＿＿＿＿＿＿＿＿＿＿＿＿＿＿＿＿＿＿＿＿

B 다음 두 문장이 같은 뜻이 되도록 빈칸에 알맞은 말을 넣어 문장을 완성하시오.

1 Hearing the news, I called Steve immediately.
→ As ＿＿＿＿＿ ＿＿＿＿＿ the news, I called Steve immediately.

2 Going to bed, I usually drink some warm water.
→ Before ＿＿＿＿＿ ＿＿＿＿＿ to bed, I usually drink some warm water.

3 I was lying on the beach while I was reading *The Great Gatsby*.
→ I was lying on the beach, ＿＿＿＿＿ *The Great Gatsby*.

4 Taking a taxi, Owen was late for the meeting.
→ Although ＿＿＿＿＿ ＿＿＿＿＿ a taxi, Owen was late for the meeting.

C 다음 밑줄 친 부분을 바르게 고쳐 쓰시오.

Hint
분사구문의 부정은 분사 앞에 not/never를 붙인다.

Not knowing how to get there, he was afraid to go by himself.
그는 그곳에 가는 법을 몰라서 혼자 가는 것을 두려워했다.

1 Before <u>went</u> to the movies, we ate dinner. → ＿＿＿＿＿

2 Telling <u>not</u> me the truth, you can't get my advice. → ＿＿＿＿＿ ＿＿＿＿＿

3 <u>Came down</u> from upstairs, Mark fell down the stairs. → ＿＿＿＿＿ ＿＿＿＿＿

4 <u>Take</u> a shower, I heard somebody knocking on the door. → ＿＿＿＿＿

Eng-Eng VOCA

slide down	to move down easily over a smooth or wet surface
pass	to succeed in an examination or test
immediately	without delay
lie	to be in a flat position on a surface
knock	to hit a door or window with your knuckles in order to get people's attention

Grammar
Lesson 3

❶ 분사구문의 시제

부사절과 주절이 같은 시제 「동사원형+-ing」	If I <u>get</u> a scholarship, I <u>can go</u> to university. → Getting a scholarship, I <u>can go</u> to university. 나는 장학금을 타면 대학에 갈 수 있다.
부사절이 주절보다 앞선 시제 「Having+p.p.」	After I <u>had arrived</u> at home, I <u>realized</u> that I left my cell phone in the library. → Having arrived at home, I <u>realized</u> that I left my cell phone in the library. 나는 집에 도착하고 나서야 전화기를 도서관에 두고 왔다는 것을 깨달았다.

❷ 수동 분사구문 Being 또는 Having been은 생략 가능

부사절과 주절이 같은 시제 「(Being)+p.p.」	When he <u>was asked</u> an unexpected question, he <u>was</u> embarrassed. → (Being) Asked an unexpected question, he <u>was</u> embarrassed. 그는 예기치 못한 질문을 받았을 때 당황했다.
부사절이 주절보다 앞선 시제 「(Having been)+p.p.」	As she <u>was born</u> and <u>raised</u> in Switzerland, she <u>speaks</u> both French and German. → (Having been) Born and raised in Switzerland, she <u>speaks</u> both French and German. 그녀는 스위스에서 나고 자라서 프랑스어와 독일어를 한다.

★ 관용 표현

❶ 독립분사구문 주어가 생략되지 않은 분사구문

<u>Snow</u> starting to fall, <u>the kids went</u> outside to make a snowman.

← When <u>snow started</u> to fall, <u>the kids went</u> outside to make a snowman.

눈이 내리기 시작하자 아이들은 눈사람을 만들러 밖으로 나갔다.

<u>There</u> being no place to sit, <u>they left</u> the room.

← Because <u>there was</u> no place to sit, <u>they left</u> the room.

그들은 앉을 곳이 없어서 방을 떠났다.

❷ 비인칭 독립분사구문 주어가 생략된 관용적인 분사구문

generally[frankly] speaking 일반적으로/솔직히 말해서	Frankly speaking, you didn't do well on the game. 솔직히 말해서 너는 그 경기에서 별로 잘하지 못했다.
judging from ~으로 판단하건대	Judging from her face, she seems very satisfied. 그녀의 표정으로 판단하건대, 그녀는 매우 만족스러운 것 같다.
speaking[talking] of ~에 관한 이야기가 나와서 말인데, ~의 이야기라면	Speaking of holidays, where do you want to go for this holiday? 휴가 이야기가 나와서 말인데, 이번 휴가에 어디로 가기를 원하니?

Practice

Answers p.04

A 다음 두 문장이 같은 뜻이 되도록 문장을 완성하시오.

1 Even though I ate dinner, I'm still hungry.

→ _____ dinner, I'm still hungry.

2 Although I was invited, I didn't go to the party.

→ _____, I didn't go to the party.

3 As I finished my homework, I have nothing to do now.

→ _____ my homework, I have nothing to do now.

4 As it was fine this morning, we went out for a walk.

→ It _____ fine this morning, we went out for a walk.

B 다음 밑줄 친 부분을 바르게 고쳐 쓰시오.

1 <u>Be</u> angry with me, Diana is not talking to me.

2 <u>Accepting</u> in the soccer club, she was very excited.

3 <u>Attended</u> the presentation, I came up with a great idea.

4 <u>Has watched</u> the weather forecast, I brought an umbrella.

5 <u>Knowing not</u> how to drive, he bought a car.

6 <u>Gone</u> to the same university, we hardly see each other.

C 다음 우리말과 같은 뜻이 되도록 주어진 단어를 이용하여 문장을 완성하시오.

1 숙제 이야기가 나와서 말인데, 마감일이 언제야? (of, speak)

_____ the assignment, when is the due date?

2 일반적으로 말해서, 사람들은 타인에 의해 쉽게 상처를 받는다. (generally, speak)

_____, people are easily hurt by others.

3 내 경험으로 판단하건대, 그들은 제시간에 도착할 수 없을 거야. (from, judge)

_____ my experience, they can't make it on time.

Eng-Eng VOCA

attend	to be present at an event
come up with	to find or produce an answer that is needed
assignment	a piece of work that is given to someone as part of their job
due date	the date by which something is supposed to happen
on time	at the correct time or the time that was arranged

VOCA
in Grammar

Answers p.04

A 다음 주어진 단어에 맞도록 의미를 바르게 연결하시오.

1 disappointing •   • a. extremely tired

2 embarrassing •   • b. feeling afraid

3 frightened •   • c. making you feel ashamed, nervous, or uncomfortable

4 exhausted •   • d. feeling annoyed and impatient about something

5 irritated •   • e. not as good as you hoped or expected

B 다음 괄호 안에서 알맞은 것을 고르시오.

1 There (having / being) no place to sit, they left the room.

2 The kid was (lighted / delighted) to see the dinosaur exhibition.

3 (While / During) attending college, Peter worked as a fashion model.

4 Frankly (speaking / talking), you didn't do well on the game.

5 Born and (rose / raised) in Switzerland, she speaks both French and German.

C 다음 〈보기〉에서 알맞은 단어를 골라 문장을 완성하시오.

| 보기 | judging | dancing | wounded | having | interesting |

1 _____ arrived at home, I realized that I left my cell phone in the library.

2 All the audience stood up, _____ to the music.

3 The kids took good care of the _____ cat.

4 _____ from her face, she seems very satisfied.

5 The English class was very _____.

24

Chapter
03
완료시제

Grammar
Lesson 1

★ 현재완료 과거에 시작된 일이 현재에도 영향을 줄 때

❶ 경험: Have you ever been to Thailand? 태국에 가본 적이 있습니까?

❷ 계속: My aunt has worked as a teacher since 2015. 우리 이모는 2015년부터 교사로 일하고 있다.

❸ 완료: Ben has just finished writing his first novel. Ben은 이제막 그의 첫 소설을 다 썼다.

❹ 결과: Amanda has lost her brand-new bike. Amanda는 새 자전거를 잃어버렸다.

★ 현재완료 vs. 과거

❶ 현재완료는 특정 과거 시점을 나타내는 말과 함께 쓸 수 없다.

현재완료	과거 시점 표현	과거
I've already eaten dinner. 나는 이미 저녁을 먹었다.	X ○	I ate dinner at 6 p.m. 나는 오후 여섯 시에 저녁을 먹었다.

❷ 과거에 시작된 일이 현재에도 영향을 줄 때는 현재완료를 쓴다.

현재완료	현재 상태와의 관련성	과거
He has lost his sunglasses. 그는 선글라스를 잃어버렸다. (여전히 못 찾은 상태)	○ X	He lost his sunglasses. 그는 선글라스를 잃어버렸다. (찾았는지 여전히 못 찾았는지 알 수 없음)

★ 현재완료진행 과거에 시작한 행동이나 상태가 현재에도 진행 중

My father has been driving for three hours. 우리 아버지는 세 시간 동안 운전을 하고 계신다.

I have been cleaning the house since this morning. 나는 오늘 아침부터 집 청소를 하고 있다.

★ 현재완료 vs. 현재완료진행

❶ 현재완료(완료) vs. 현재완료진행

현재완료(완료)	동작	현재완료진행
She has just read the newspaper. 그녀는 방금 신문을 읽었다. (동작 완료)	완료 계속	She has been reading the newspaper. 그녀는 신문을 읽고 있다. (동작 계속)

❷ 현재완료(계속) vs. 현재완료진행 의미의 차이가 거의 없음

현재완료(계속)	동작	현재완료진행
She has lived in China for ten years. 그녀는 중국에서 10년 동안 살고 있다.	계속 계속	She has been living in China for ten years. 그녀는 중국에서 10년 동안 살고 있다.

Practice

Answers p.05

A 다음 두 문장이 같은 뜻이 되도록 문장을 완성하시오.

1 Jamie left his wallet on his desk. It's still there.

→ Jamie _____ _____ his wallet on his desk.

2 I began to live with my cousins last year. I still live with them.

→ I _____ _____ with my cousins since last year.

3 We started learning Japanese three years ago. We still learn Japanese.

→ We _____ _____ Japanese for three years.

B 다음 주어진 단어를 이용하여 대화를 완성하시오.

1 A: _____ you ever _____ (see) a real snake?

B: Sure. I _____ (see) one at the zoo three days ago.

2 A: Last winter, I _____ (go) skiing for the first time.

B: Really? I _____ _____ (ski) several times.

3 A: I'm so happy. I _____ just _____ (finish) my homework.

B: You were quick. You _____ (start) thirty minutes ago.

4 A: I _____ _____ (call) him twice, but there's no answer.

B: That's strange. I _____ (call) him two hours ago, and he answered.

C 다음 〈보기〉에서 알맞은 동사를 골라 현재완료진행으로 바꿔 문장을 완성하시오.

> **보기**   play   take   work   rain   study   live

1 I _____ _____ _____ Chinese since 2016.

2 She _____ _____ _____ in Seoul for three years.

3 My niece _____ _____ _____ a nap for two hours.

4 Ralph _____ _____ _____ as a photographer for ten years.

5 It _____ _____ _____ since last night.

6 The children _____ _____ _____ in the garden since lunch time.

Eng-Eng VOCA

cousin	the child of your uncle or aunt
several	more than two but not very many
strange	unusual or surprising, especially in a way that is difficult to explain or understand
niece	the daughter of your brother or sister
take a nap	to sleep for a short period of time during the day

Grammar
Lesson 2

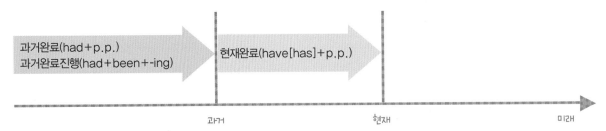

I found that I **had left** my notebook at home when I opened my bag.
나는 가방을 열어보고 공책을 집에 놓고 온 것을 알았다.

When I woke up this morning, my sister **had** already **gone** to school.
내가 오늘 아침에 깼을 때 내 여동생은 이미 학교에 가고 없었다.

Eric had **worked** at the company for thirty years when I met him.
내가 Eric을 만났을 때 Eric은 그 회사에서 30년 동안 일을 해왔다.

Bella had never **been** to a foreign country before she became a fashion model.
Bella는 패션모델이 되기 전에는 한 번도 외국에 가본 적이 없었다.

★ 과거완료와 과거

Joe **missed** the school bus because he **had overslept**. Joe는 늦잠을 자서 스쿨버스를 놓쳤다.
　　　나중에 일어난 일(과거)　　　　　　　　　　　　먼저 일어난 일(과거완료: 대과거)

Sam **had read** books about Japan before he **visited** Tokyo. Sam은 도쿄를 방문하기 전에 일본에 관한 책을 읽었다.
　　먼저 일어난 일(과거완료: 대과거)　　　　　　나중에 일어난 일(과거)

★ 과거완료진행

Rachel **had been teaching** at the college for more than ten years before she left for America.
Rachel은 미국으로 떠나기 전에 10년 이상 그 대학에서 강의를 했다.

Becky and Jessica **had been talking** for almost an hour when they heard a strange sound.
Becky와 Jessica가 이상한 소리를 들었을 때 그들은 거의 한 시간 동안 이야기를 하고 있었다.

* 과거완료는 과거에 일어난 일들의 선후관계를 나타내는 데 이용되며, 과거완료진행은 특정한 과거 시점 이전에 시작된 일이 그 특정 과거 시점까지
　진행 중임을 나타낼 때 쓴다.

Practice

Answers p.05

A 다음 주어진 동사를 현재완료 또는 과거완료로 바꿔 문장을 완성하시오.

1 _____ you _____ (clean) your room?

2 I _____ already _____ (know) him when Maggie introduced him to me.

3 Alice _____ (buy) a new shirt, and she is wearing it now.

4 When we arrived at the airport, the plane _____ (take off).

5 The Palace of Versailles was more luxurious than I _____ (imagine).

6 My brother _____ (do) his homework when I got home.

B 다음 〈보기〉와 같이 주어진 동사를 과거와 과거완료로 바꿔 문장을 완성하시오.

> **보기** After Vicky ____had graduated____ (graduate) from university,
> she ____worked____ (work) as an engineer.

1 The coffee _____ (go) cold by the time I _____ (take) a sip.

2 Phillip _____ (live) in Paris before he _____ (move) to Rome.

3 The game _____ already _____ (finish) when it _____ (begin) to rain.

4 Joseph and Anna _____ (chat) online many times before they first _____ (meet) in person.

C 다음 〈보기〉에서 알맞은 동사를 골라 과거완료진행으로 바꿔 문장을 완성하시오.

> **보기**   play   drive   study   sleep

1 Alex _____ for almost ten hours when I woke him up.

2 Noah _____ for three hours before he left the library.

3 By the time he arrived, Nick _____ for more than 8 hours.

4 The children _____ for several hours when their mother called them.

Eng-Eng VOCA	
graduate from	to complete a course in education at a school or college
engineer	someone who designs or builds roads, bridges, or machines
take a sip	to take a small amount of a drink into your mouth
in person	actually present at a place
wake up	to make someone stop sleeping

A 다음 주어진 단어에 맞도록 의미를 바르게 연결하시오.

1 leave •   • a. to no longer have something because you do not know where it is

2 visit •   • b. to feel sad that a person or thing is not present

3 miss •   • c. to not take something or someone with you when you go

4 stay •   • d. to go and spend time in a place or with someone

5 lose •   • e. to remain in the same place

B 다음 괄호 안에서 알맞은 것을 고르시오.

1 She has been (read / reading) the newspaper.

2 Ben has just (finish / finished) writing his first novel.

3 Rachel has (teaching / taught) at the college for more than ten years.

4 When I work up this morning, my sister had already (went / gone) to school.

5 How long have you (been / being) waiting for me here?

C 다음 〈보기〉에서 알맞은 단어를 골라 문장을 완성하시오.

| 보기 | ever | for | since | yet | already |

1 Robin hasn't arrived at the airport _____.

2 I have been cleaning the house _____ this morning.

3 Have you _____ been to Thailand?

4 I have _____ eaten dinner.

5 My father has been driving _____ three hours.

Chapter
04
수동태

Grammar
Lesson 1

★ 수동태의 의미와 형태

❶ 수동태의 의미 동작을 당하는 대상, '~당하다, ~하여지다'

English **is spoken** all around the world. 영어는 전 세계에서 쓰인다.

A lot of money **is spent** around Christmas time. 크리스마스 때는 많은 돈이 소비된다.

❷ 능동태와 수동태의 구분

▷ 능동태와 수동태를 바르게 이용하려면 문장의 의미를 파악하는 것이 가장 중요하다. 능동태는 주어가 동작을 행하는 주체가 되고, 수동태는 주어가 동작을 당하는 대상이 된다.

Bell **invented** the telephone. Bell이 전화기를 발명했다.

(×) Bell was invented by the telephone.
　　Bell이 전화기에 의해 발명될 수는 없으므로 문장이 성립하지 않는다.

The telephone **was invented** by Bell. 전화기가 Bell에 의해 발명되었다.

(×) The telephone invented Bell.
　　전화기가 Bell을 발명할 수는 없으므로 문장이 성립하지 않는다.

❸ 수동태로 전환

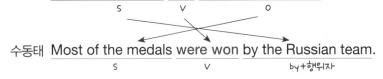

능동태 The Russian team won most of the medals. 러시아 팀이 메달의 대부분을 획득했다.
　　　　S　　　　　　　V　　　O

수동태 Most of the medals were won by the Russian team.
　　　　S　　　　　　　V　　　by+행위자

❹ 수동태의 형태

시제	형태	예문
미래	will + be + p.p.	The paintings will be displayed next month. 그 그림들은 다음 달에 전시될 것입니다. The package will be delivered by this Friday. 소포는 이번 금요일까지 배달될 것입니다.
현재 과거	be동사 + p.p.	Kimchi is eaten by most Koreans. 한국사람 대부분이 김치를 먹는다. The 2016 Summer Olympic Games were held in Rid de Janeiro. 2016 하계 올림픽이 리우데자네이루에서 개최되었다.
진행	be동사 + being + p.p.	He is being followed by his fans. 그의 팬들이 그를 따라다니고 있다. His idea was being considered carefully at that time. 그 당시에는 그의 의견이 조심스럽게 고려되고 있었다.
완료	have [has / had] + been + p.p.	The building has been built by a Korean company. 그 건물은 한국 회사에 의해 지어졌다. She was happy because her offer had been accepted. 그녀는 자신의 제안이 받아들여져서 기뻤다.

Practice

Answers p.06

A 다음 문장을 수동태로 바꿔 쓰시오.

1 Jasper invited me to the wedding.

→ I _____ to the wedding by Jasper.

2 Alice's mother is making her sweater.

→ Alice's sweater _____ by her mother.

3 A reporter at the Korea Times wrote that article.

→ That article _____ by a reporter at the Korea Times.

4 My brother has broken my computer several times.

→ My computer _____ several times by my brother.

Plus

수동태로 쓰지 않는 동사

① 목적어를 갖지 않는 동사: appear, become, disappear, happen 등

Suddenly, Amy appeared on stage. (was appeared)
Amy가 갑자기 무대에 나타났다.

② 목적어가 있어도 수동태로 쓰지 않는 동사: cost(비용이 ~들다), have(소유하다), resemble(닮다) 등

It cost me a lot of money. (was cost)
그것은 비쌌다.

B 다음 밑줄 친 부분을 바르게 고쳐 쓰시오.

1 Antique furniture <u>usually makes</u> of wood.

2 My house <u>built</u> by my grandfather ten years ago.

3 The new student <u>introduced</u> to the class by the teacher.

4 My brother <u>has been worked</u> at a hospital since he graduated from university.

5 The kids <u>told</u> to be quiet by their parents.

6 This website <u>designs</u> by my sister a year ago.

C 다음 우리말과 같은 뜻이 되도록 주어진 동사를 이용하여 문장을 완성하시오.

1 우리 마을에 있는 병원은 3년 전에 지어졌다.

→ The hospital in my town _____ (build) three years ago.

2 이 책들은 도서관에 반납되어야 합니다.

→ These books should _____ (return) to the library.

3 매년 동물원에서 많은 고기가 사자와 호랑이에 의해 소비된다.

→ Every year, a lot of meat _____ (consume) by lions and tigers at the zoo.

Eng-Eng VOCA

invite	to ask someone to come to an event like a party and wedding
wedding	a ceremony at which two people are married to each other
article	a piece of writing about a subject in a newspaper or magazine
antique	old and valuable
consume	to eat or drink something; to use fuel, energy or time

Grammar
Lesson 2

모바일단어장

★ **4문형의 수동태** 〔주어+동사+간접목적어+직접목적어〕

❶ 목적어가 두 개인 문장은 두 가지 형태의 수동태를 만들 수 있다.

Jim gave <u>me</u> <u>a glass of cold water</u>. Jim이 나에게 찬물 한 잔을 주었다.
　　　　①간·목(IO)　　②직·목(DO)

| ① 간접목적어가 주어인 경우 | I <u>was given</u> a glass of cold water by Jim. |
| ② 직접목적어가 주어인 경우 | A glass of cold water <u>was given</u> to me by Jim. |

❷ 직접목적어를 주어로 하여 수동태 문장을 만들 때는 간접목적어 앞에 전치사(to, for, of)를 쓴다.

for를 쓰는 동사	buy, cook, get, make 등
to를 쓰는 동사	bring, give, lend, show, teach, tell 등
of를 쓰는 동사	ask

My father bought me **a pair of boots**. 우리 아버지가 나에게 부츠 한 켤레를 사 주셨다.

→ A pair of boots <u>was bought</u> for me by my father.

We will show them **the design** for the new car at the meeting. 우리는 회의에서 신차 디자인을 그들에게 보여줄 것이다.

→ The design for the new car will <u>be shown</u> to them at the meeting (by us).

★ **5문형의 수동태** 〔주어+동사+목적어+목적격보어〕

❶ 목적어를 주어로 하여 수동태를 만든다. 목적격보어를 주어로 하여 수동태를 만들 수 없다.

We elected **Julia** class president. 우리가 Julia를 반장으로 선출했다.

→ Julia <u>was elected</u> class president (by us).
~~Class president was elected Julia (by us).~~ (X)

❷ 목적격보어가 분사인 경우 분사를 그대로 쓴다.

I <u>saw</u> **Maria** talking to her teacher this morning. 나는 오늘 아침에 Maria가 선생님에게 이야기하고 있는 것을 보았다.

→ Maria <u>was seen</u> talking to her teacher this morning (by me).

❸ 목적격보어가 동사원형인 경우 동사원형 앞에 **to**를 쓴다.

My father <u>made</u> **me** water the plants in the garden. 우리 아버지가 나에게 정원에 있는 나무에 물을 주도록 시켰다.

→ I <u>was made</u> to water the plants in the garden by my father.

Practice

Answers p.06

A 다음 괄호 안에서 알맞은 것을 고르시오.

1 We (told / were told) what to do next by our teacher.

2 My sister and I (made / were made) to clean our room.

3 A baby koala (observed / was observed) sleeping in the tree.

4 My favorite meals (always make / are always made) by my mother.

B 다음 문장을 수동태로 바꿔 쓰시오.

1 Carolyn taught me how to swim.

→ I ＿＿＿＿＿ ＿＿＿＿＿＿＿＿＿＿ how to swim by Carolyn.

2 Tommy showed me his secret place.

→ I ＿＿＿＿＿＿＿＿＿＿＿＿＿＿ Tommy's secret place by him.

→ Tommy's secret place ＿＿＿＿＿＿＿＿＿＿＿＿ me by him.

3 My family gave me a birthday present.

→ I ＿＿＿＿＿＿＿＿＿＿＿＿＿＿ a birthday present by my family.

→ A birthday present ＿＿＿＿＿＿＿＿＿＿＿ me by my family.

4 Bella's parents bought her these in-line skates.

→ These in-line skates ＿＿＿＿＿＿＿＿＿＿ Bella by her parents.

> **plus**
> buy, make 등의 동사는 주로 직접 목적어를 주어로 하여 수동태 문장을 만든다.
> He bought me a cell phone.
> 그가 나에게 휴대전화를 사 주었다.
> → A cell phone was bought for me by him. (O)
> → ~~I was bought a cell phone by him.~~ (X)

C 다음 문장을 수동태로 바꿔 쓰시오.

1 We call him Uncle Bob.

→ He ＿＿＿＿＿＿＿＿＿＿＿＿＿＿＿＿ by us.

2 He made me return the books.

→ I ＿＿＿＿＿＿＿＿＿＿＿＿＿＿＿ the books by him.

3 Steven kept me waiting for an hour.

→ I ＿＿＿＿＿＿＿＿＿＿＿＿＿＿＿ for an hour by Steven.

4 We watched some deer eating the grass.

→ Some deer ＿＿＿＿＿＿＿＿＿＿＿＿＿＿＿＿＿ the grass by us.

> **Eng-Eng VOCA**
>
> | | |
> |---|---|
> | observe | to watch someone/something to learn more about them |
> | secret | kept hidden from others |
> | place | a particular space or area |
> | return | to give or send something back, or to put something back in its place |
> | keep | to cause someone/something to do something continuously or again and again |

Grammar
Lesson 3

1 수동태의 행위자는 일반적으로 「by＋행위자」로 쓰지만, by 대신 다른 전치사를 쓰기도 한다.

be amazed at[by] ~에 놀라다	be covered with[by, in] ~으로 덮여 있다
be crowded with ~으로 붐비다	be disappointed with[at, about, by] ~에 실망하다
be filled with ~으로 가득 차 있다	be frightened of ~에 겁나다
be interested in ~에 관심이 있다	be married to ~와 결혼하다
be pleased with[at] ~에 기뻐하다	be satisfied with ~에 만족하다
be shocked at[by] ~에 충격을 받다	be surprised at[by] ~에 놀라다

All the furniture **was covered with** white cloth. 모든 가구가 흰 천으로 덮여 있었다.

The amusement park is always **crowded with** kids and parents on Children's day.
어린이날에 놀이공원은 항상 아이들과 부모로 붐빈다.

2 전치사에 따라 다른 의미를 갖기도 한다.

be known for ~으로 유명하다   be known as ~로 알려져 있다   be known by ~로 알 수 있다
be known to＋명사 ~에게 알려져 있다   be known to＋동사원형 ~로 알려져 있다

He is **known for** his good looks. 그는 잘 생긴 외모로 유명하다.

She is **known as** a writer. 그녀는 작가로 알려져 있다.

A man is **known by** the company he keeps. ((속담)) 사람은 친구를 보면 알 수 있다.

The scientist is **known to** everybody. 그 과학자는 모두에게 알려져 있다.

They are **known to** be interested in modern art. 그들은 현대 미술에 관심이 있는 것으로 알려져 있다.

be made of (물리적 변화) ~으로 만들어지다   be made from (화학적 변화) ~으로 만들어지다

Those bottles **are made of** glass. 이 병들은 유리로 만들어졌다.

Paper **is made from** wood. 종이는 나무로 만들어진다.

3 동사구는 하나의 동사처럼 취급하여 수동태 문장을 만든다.

bring up ~을 기르다, 양육하다	call off ~을 취소하다	carry out ~을 실행하다
laugh at ~을 비웃다	look after ~을 돌보다	look up to ~을 존경하다
put on ~을 입다	put off ~을 미루다	run over ~을 (차로) 치다
send for ~을 부르러 보내다	take care of ~을 돌보다	take off ~을 벗다
turn off ~을 끄다	turn on ~을 켜다	

They **called off** the trip to Australia. 그들이 호주 여행을 취소했다.

→ The trip to Australia **was called off** by them.

My sister will **take care of** my cat while I'm on vacation. 내 휴가 기간 동안 내 여동생이 내 고양이를 돌봐줄 것이다.

→ My cat will **be taken care of** by my sister while I'm on vacation.

Practice

Answers p.06

A 다음 괄호 안에서 알맞은 것을 고르시오.

1 The small boxes were filled (of / with) children's books.

2 The floor in my room was covered (at / with) newspapers.

3 The theater was crowded (at / with) reporters and fans.

4 She was surprised (at / to) the amount of work that she has to do.

5 Mike is interested (in / of) learning foreign languages.

B 다음 밑줄 친 부분을 바르게 고쳐 쓰시오.

1 Paulo is <u>known to</u> his outstanding writing style.

2 My best friend is <u>married with</u> my younger sister.

3 Nancy's grandmother has been <u>looked after</u> Nancy.

4 The company was <u>satisfied at</u> the work that he's done.

5 The kid was <u>laughed at</u> her classmates.

C 다음 우리말과 같은 뜻이 되도록 주어진 단어를 이용하여 문장을 완성하시오.

1 나는 그의 이기적인 행동에 실망했다. (disappoint)

→ I _____ with his selfish behavior.

2 Brian의 부모님은 그의 발전에 기뻐했다. (please)

→ Brian's parents _____ with his progress.

3 학생들은 담임선생님의 보살핌을 받고 있다. (take care of)

→ The students _____ by their homeroom teacher.

4 그들은 행사에 참여한 사람들의 수에 놀랐다. (surprise)

→ They _____ at the number of people who participated in the event.

Eng-Eng VOCA

outstanding	extremely good or excellent
look after	to take care of someone by helping them
selfish	caring only about yourself and not about other people
behavior	the way a person or animal acts
progress	the process of improving or developing

VOCA
in Grammar

Answers p.07

A 다음 주어진 단어에 맞도록 의미를 바르게 연결하시오.

1 elect •
2 consider •
3 display •
4 cover •
5 invent •

• a. to think of someone or something in a particular way or to have a particular opinion

• b. to design or create something that has never been made before

• c. to put or spread something over something

• d. to choose a person for a particular job, by voting

• e. to arrange something or a collection of things so that it can be seen by the public

B 다음 괄호 안에서 알맞은 것을 고르시오.

1 The trip to Australia was (called of / called off) by them.

2 The teacher was (looked up to / seen up to) by my friends.

3 The soccer game was (put off / pulled off) because of bad weather.

4 The poor deer was (run on / run over) by a car.

5 My dog will be (looked before / looked after) by the vet.

C 다음 〈보기〉에서 알맞은 단어를 골라 문장을 완성하시오.

| 보기 | for | at | of | with | from |

1 Paper is made _____ wood.

2 Those bottles are made _____ glass.

3 He is known _____ his good looks.

4 All the furniture was covered _____ white cloth.

5 I was shocked _____ my brother's behavior.

Chapter

05

조동사

Grammar
Lesson 1

★ used to 관련 표현

❶ 「used to+동사원형」

과거의 행동이나 상태 「used to+동사원형」 「would+동사원형」	My father used to drive my sister and me to school. → My father would drive my sister and me to school. <small>우리 아버지는 언니와 나를 학교에 데려다 주시곤 하셨다.</small>
과거의 상태 「used to+동사원형」	When I was younger, there used to be a big apple tree in the backyard. <small>내가 어렸을 때 뒷마당에 큰 사과나무가 있었다.</small>

* '~하곤 했었다'라는 의미로 과거의 반복적인 행동이나 지속적인 상태를 나타낼 때 쓰며, 지금은 그렇지 않다는 뜻을 포함한다.
과거의 행동을 나타낼 때는 「would+동사원형」으로 바꿔 쓸 수 있다.

❷ be used to

「be[get] used to+-ing」 ~하는 데 익숙하다, 익숙해지다	He should be used to getting up early. <small>그는 일찍 일어나는 데 익숙해져야 한다.</small> She got used to living in a big city. <small>그녀는 큰 도시에 사는 것에 익숙해졌다.</small>
「be used to+동사원형」 ~하는 데 이용되다 (수동태)	Many different kinds of wood are used to make pianos. <small>많은 종류의 나무가 피아노를 만드는 데 사용된다.</small> This cloth will be used to cover the old furniture. <small>이 천은 오래된 가구를 덮는 데 이용될 것이다.</small>

★ can 관련 표현

「cannot help -ing」 =「cannot but+동사원형」 ~하지 않을 수 없다	He could not help thinking about her. <small>그는 그녀에 대해 생각하지 않을 수가 없었다.</small> I cannot but agree with you. <small>나는 너에게 동의하지 않을 수 없다.</small>
「cannot+동사원형 +too+형용사」 아무리 ~해도 지나치지 않다	We cannot be too careful when driving a car. <small>차를 운전할 때는 아무리 조심해도 지나치지 않다.</small>

★ may 관련 표현

「may[might] as well +동사원형」 ~하는 편이 좋겠다	If you don't need me anymore, I may as well leave now. <small>더 이상 내가 필요 없으면 나는 이제 떠나는 편이 좋겠다.</small> You may as well tell your score to your parents. <small>너는 부모님께 점수를 말씀 드리는 편이 좋겠다.</small>
「may well+동사원형」 ~하는 것도 당연하다. 아마 ~일 것이다	You may well say so. <small>네가 그렇게 말하는 것도 당연하다.</small> He may well be right. <small>그가 맞을지도 모른다.</small>

Practice

Answers p.07

A 다음 괄호 안에서 알맞은 것을 고르시오.

1 This knife (used to / is used to) cut bread only.

2 When I was a child, I (used to / was used to) live in the countryside.

3 My father (used to / was used to) read books to me when I was young.

4 When I lived in New York, I (used to / was used to) jog in Central Park.

5 Ice is used to (build / building) shelter for some native people of the Arctic.

6 Gary was used to (play / playing) by himself because he's an only child.

B 다음 주어진 단어를 알맞은 형태로 바꿔 문장을 완성하시오.

1 We are used to _____ (walk) two kilometers to school.

2 When I was a child, I used to _____ (enjoy) fishing on weekends.

3 A thermometer is used to _____ (measure) the temperature of the air.

4 My family used to _____ (go) camping in the summer when I was in school.

5 I will never get used to _____ (get) up at 5 a.m.

6 My parents would _____ (watch) a movie on Friday nights.

C 다음 우리말과 같은 뜻이 되도록 문장을 완성하시오.

1 그의 농담에 웃지 않을 수가 없다. (laugh, at)

　→ I _____ _____ _____ _____ his joke.

　→ I _____ _____ _____ _____ his joke.

2 내가 전에 너에게 거짓말을 했으니, 네가 그렇게 생각하는 것도 당연해. (think)

　→ I lied to you before, so you _____ _____ _____ that way.

3 너는 그들에게 지금 말하는 편이 좋겠어. 그들이 조만간 알아낼 거야. (tell)

　→ You _____ _____ _____ _____ them now. They'll find out
　sooner or later.

Eng-Eng VOCA

countryside	land that is outside cities and towns
shelter	a place to live; a structure that protects people or things
only child	a child who has no brothers or sisters
thermometer	a device for measuring temperature
measure	to find out the size, length, or amount of something

Grammar
Lesson 2

❶ 추측(과거)

「must have p.p.」 ~했음에 틀림없다	He must have left already. His car is gone. 그는 이미 떠났음에 틀림없어. 그의 차가 없어. She must have forgotten to turn off her computer. Her computer is still on. 그녀가 컴퓨터 끄는 것을 잊어버렸음에 틀림없어. 그녀의 컴퓨터가 아직도 켜져 있어.
「must not have p.p.」 ~하지 않았음에 틀림없다	She must not[mustn't] have heard you. She was listening to music loud then. 그녀가 네 말을 듣지 못했음에 틀림없어. 그녀는 그때 음악을 크게 듣고 있었어. He mustn't have seen me. He didn't say "hello" to me when he passed by. 그가 나를 보지 못했음에 틀림없어. 내 옆을 지나갈 때 나에게 '안녕'이라고 인사하지 않았어.
「cannot have p.p.」 ~했을 리가 없다	He cannot have finished his homework. He just started to do it. 그는 숙제를 끝냈을 리가 없어. 그는 막 그것을 하기 시작했어. He cannot have read that book. He can't read Russian. 그가 저 책을 읽었을 리가 없어. 그는 러시아어를 읽을 줄 몰라.
「may[might] have p.p.」 ~했을지도 모른다	They may have seen each other before. 그들은 전에 서로 본적이 있었을지도 몰라. She didn't answer the phone. She might have left her phone at home. 그녀가 전화를 받지 않았어. 아마 전화기를 집에 놓고 갔을지도 몰라.

❷ 유감

「should have p.p.」 ~했어야 했다 (하지 않았다)	I should have bought the tickets last night. The concert is completely sold out. 나는 어젯밤에 표를 샀어야 했다. 그 콘서트가 완전히 매진되었다. Richard shouldn't have gone to bed so late. He looks really tired today. Richard는 밤에 그렇게 늦게 자지 않았어야 했다. 그는 오늘 정말 피곤해 보인다.
「could have p.p.」 ~할 수 있었다 (하지 못했다)	Why didn't you ask me? I could have gone with you. 왜 나에게 부탁하지 않았어? 내가 너와 함께 갈 수도 있었는데. I could have driven you to school. 나는 너를 학교에 데려다 줄 수도 있었는데.

* 「조동사＋have＋p.p.」는 주로 가정법의 주절에 이용되어 '~할 수도 있었는데 하지 않았다'라는 의미로 쓰인다.

Practice

Answers p.07

A 다음 주어진 단어를 이용하여 문장을 완성하시오.

1 They are not at home. They _____ (may, go) to the movies.

2 I _____ (should, take) the subway. I'm stuck in heavy traffic.

3 She won first prize. She _____ (must, practice) very hard.

4 Kelly was in a bad mood. You _____ (could, warn) me not to make fun of her.

B 다음 〈보기〉에서 알맞은 동사를 골라 주어진 조동사를 이용하여 문장을 완성하시오.

| 보기 | lose | put | pick up | return |

1 Cindy _____ (should) John at the airport, but she didn't.

2 Tim _____ (must, not) from vacation. I didn't see him all day.

3 She _____ (should, not) that much sugar in the pumpkin pie. It's too sweet.

4 They _____ (must) our bags. All the luggage from our flight has already come out, except for ours.

C 다음 우리말과 같은 뜻이 되도록 주어진 단어를 이용하여 문장을 완성하시오.

1 도로가 젖어 있다. 비가 내렸음에 틀림없다. (must, rain)

→ The road is wet. It _____.

2 내가 샤워를 하고 있을 때, 그녀가 내게 전화를 했을지도 모른다. (may, call)

→ She _____ me when I was taking a shower.

3 그가 그 일을 혼자 해결했을 리가 없다. 그것은 간단한 문제가 아니었다. (can, solve)

→ He _____ the problem by himself. It wasn't a simple problem.

4 나는 커피를 마시지 않았어야 했다. 나는 지금 잠을 잘 수가 없다. (should, drink)

→ I _____ coffee. I cannot sleep now.

Eng-Eng VOCA

stuck	in a place or situation that is difficult to get out of
traffic	the vehicles that are on a road
make fun of	to make a joke about someone or something in an unkind way
luggage	the bags and suitcases that a person carries when traveling
solve	to find a way of dealing with a problem

VOCA in Grammar

Answers p.08

A 다음 주어진 단어가 문장의 빈칸에 알맞게 들어가도록 연결하시오.

1　must　•

2　cannot　•

3　could　•

4　should　•

5　might　•

• a. He _____ have finished his homework. He just started to do it.

• b. They both graduated from Harvard. They _____ have seen each other on campus.

• c. She _____ have forgotten to turn off her computer. Her computer is still on.

• d. Why didn't you ask me? I _____ have gone with you.

• e. I _____ have bought the tickets last night. The concert is completely sold out.

B 다음 괄호 안에서 알맞은 것을 고르시오.

1　There (would / used to) be a big apple tree in the backyard.

2　She got (use to / used to) living in a big city.

3　This cloth will be used to (cover / covering) the old furniture.

4　My father (uses to / used to) drive my sister and me to school.

5　He should get (used to / using to) getting up early.

C 다음 〈보기〉에서 알맞은 단어를 골라 문장을 완성하시오.

보기	as	but	too	well	not

1　I cannot _____ agree with you.

2　You may _____ say so.

3　He could _____ help thinking about her.

4　We cannot be _____ careful when driving a car.

5　You might _____ well tell your score to your parents.

Chapter
06
비교

Grammar
Lesson 1

❶ 「A 비교급 than B」 A가 B보다 더 ~하다

Cindy's computer is **better than** Daniel's computer. Cindy의 컴퓨터는 Daniel의 것보다 좋다.

Fred plays the drums **better than** George (does). Fred가 George보다 드럼을 잘 친다.

❷ 비교의 대상은 동등한 것이어야 한다.

The size of Russia is **larger than** that of Korea. 러시아의 크기는 한국의 크기보다 크다.

My room is **bigger than** my brother's. 내 방은 내 남동생의 방보다 크다.

(X) ~~My room is bigger than my brother.~~ 내 방과 내 동생을 비교하면 안 된다.

❸ 「A less 원급 than B」 A가 B보다 덜 ~하다

My cat is **less heavy than** his cat. 내 고양이는 그의 고양이보다 덜 무겁다.

He was probably **less lucky than** you. 그는 아마 너보다 운이 없었을 것이다.

❹ 비교급을 강조할 때는 much, still, far, even, a lot 등을 이용한다.

The lake was **much** <u>bigger</u> than I expected. 그 호수는 내가 예상했던 것보다 훨씬 컸다.

She has **a lot** <u>more</u> shoes than I do. 그녀는 나보다 훨씬 많은 신발을 가지고 있다.

❺ 「the 비교급, the 비교급」 ~하면 할수록 더 ~하다

The longer I look at the picture, the more I like it. 그 그림을 보면 볼수록 나는 그 그림을 더 좋아하게 된다.

The harder you study, the better grades you get. 네가 공부를 하면 할수록 더 좋은 성적을 얻게 된다.

❻ 「비교급 and 비교급」 점점 더, 더욱더

More and more people go traveling abroad. 점점 더 많은 사람들이 해외여행을 간다.

After the rain, it's getting colder and colder. 비가 온 이후로 점점 추워지고 있다.

❼ than 대신 to를 쓰는 비교급 표현

similar to ~와 비슷한	senior to ~보다 나이 든, 높은
prior to ~보다 앞서	junior to ~보다 어린, 낮은
inferior to ~보다 낮은, 떨어지는	superior to ~보다 우수한

My father's age is similar to his father's age. 우리 아버지와 그의 아버지는 나이가 비슷하다.

It is wrong to say one language is superior to another. 특정한 언어가 다른 언어보다 우월하다고 말하는 것은 잘못됐다.

Practice

Answers p.08

A 다음 주어진 단어를 이용하여 〈보기〉와 같이 문장을 완성하시오.

> **보기** The laptop is $1,000. The tablet PC is $500. (expensive)
> → The laptop is ___more expensive___ than the tablet PC.
> → The tablet PC is ___less expensive___ than the laptop.

1 Proposal A got 76 votes. Proposal B got 82 votes. (favored)
  → Proposal B is _____ than Proposal A.
  → Proposal A is _____ than Proposal B.

2 Mark went to bed at 9 p.m. Jacob went to bed at 11 p.m. (early)
  → Mark went to bed _____ than Jacob.
  → Jacob went to bed _____ than Mark.

B 다음 밑줄 친 부분을 어법에 맞게 고쳐 쓰시오.

1 Kids could be much <u>happy</u> than adults.

2 Amelia's cell phone is much newer than <u>me</u>.

3 My room is <u>very</u> neater than my sister's room.

4 I think this black sofa is inferior <u>than</u> that brown sofa.

> **Hint**
> 비교급 강조에는 **very**를 쓸 수 없다.
> (O) A chimpanzee is <u>much</u> smarter than a dog.
> (X) A chimpanzee is <s>very</s> smarter than a dog.
> 침팬지는 개보다 훨씬 똑똑하다.

C 다음 우리말과 같은 뜻이 되도록 주어진 단어를 이용하여 문장을 완성하시오.

1 나는 겨울보다 여름을 좋아한다. (prefer)
  → I _____ summer _____ winter.

2 기온이 점점 낮아지고 있었다. (low)
  → The temperature was getting _____ _____ _____.

3 그 문제는 생각보다 덜 복잡했다. (complicated)
  → The problem was _____ _____ than I thought.

4 그것에 대해 생각하면 할수록 나는 더 우울해졌다. (much)
  → _____ _____ I thought about it, _____ _____
  I became depressed.

> **Hint**
> 「prefer A to B」
> B보다 A를 선호하다
> I prefer walking fast <u>to</u> running.
> 나는 뛰는 것보다 빨리 걷는 것을 선호한다.

Eng-Eng VOCA

proposal	a formal suggestion or plan to be considered
favored	chosen or preferred by many people
inferior	not good or not as good as someone/something else
prefer	to like one thing or person better than another
complicated	difficult to understand; made of many different parts

Grammar
Lesson 2

★ 원급을 이용한 표현

❶ 「A as+원급+as B」 A는 B만큼 ~하다

My brother's shoes are **as big as** my father's (are). 우리 오빠의 신발은 우리 아버지의 신발만큼 크다.

The speaker talks **as fast as** my teacher (does). 그 연설가는 우리 선생님만큼 빨리 말한다.

❷ 「A not as[so]+원급+as B」 A는 B만큼 ~하지 않다

Your bag is **not as[so] heavy as** his bag (is). 네 가방은 그의 가방만큼 무겁지 않다.

Kelly doesn't jump **as[so] high as** Paul (does). Kelly는 Paul만큼 높이 뛰지 못한다.

▷ 비교급의 문장 전환

> Your bag is not as heavy as his bag.
> → His bag is heavier than your bag.
> → Your bag is less heavy than his bag.

> Kelly doesn't jump as high as Paul.
> → Paul jumps higher than Kelly.
> → Kelly jumps less high than Paul.

❸ 「A 배수사+as+원급+as B」 A는 B보다 ~배 …하다

The Sun's diameter is about 100 times **as long as** that of the Earth.
→ The Sun's diameter is about 100 times **longer than** that of the Earth.
　　태양의 지름은 지구의 지름보다 약 100배만큼 길다.

This small wheel spins three times **as fast as** that large wheel.
→ This small wheel spins three times **faster than** that large wheel.
　　이 작은 바퀴는 저 큰 바퀴보다 세 배 빠르게 돈다.

❹ 「as+원급+as possible」 = 「as+원급+as one can」 가능한 한 ~하게

Please give it back to me **as soon as possible**. 가능한 한 빨리 돌려주세요.
→ Please give it back to me **as soon as you can**.

He spoke **as quietly as possible**. 그는 가능한 한 조용하게 말했다.
→ He spoke **as quietly as he could**.

Practice

Answers p.08

A 다음 주어진 단어와 「as ~ as」를 이용하여 문장을 완성하시오.

Hint
「as many[much]+명사+as」
~만큼 많이
I ate as many cookies as my sister (did).
나는 내 여동생만큼 과자를 많이 먹었다.

1 Brian has seen _____ Jessica. (many movies)

2 Italian food is _____ Japanese food in Seoul. (popular)

3 Driving, while using a cell phone, is _____ driving after drinking alcohol. (dangerous)

4 I don't usually eat _____ Rachel. (much)

5 The living room isn't _____ the kitchen. (messy)

B 다음 〈보기〉와 같이 두 문장이 같은 뜻이 되도록 문장을 완성하시오.

> 보기 My bike is not as light as Andrew's.
> → Andrew's bike is ___lighter than___ mine.

1 Sparrows don't fly as fast as eagles.
  → Eagles fly _____ sparrows.

2 The police station is not as far as the fire station.
  → The fire station is _____ the police station.

3 Carl's new novel is not as interesting as his previous novel.
  → Carl's previous novel is _____ his new novel.

C 다음 우리말과 같은 뜻이 되도록 주어진 단어를 이용하여 문장을 완성하시오.

Hint
twice: 두 번, 두 배
three times: 세 번, 세 배
four times: 네 번, 네 배

1 그는 가능한 한 크게 말했다.
  → He spoke _____. (as, possible, loudly)
  → He spoke _____. (as, can, loudly)

2 지구는 달보다 네 배 크다.
  → The Earth is _____ the Moon. (as, big)
  → The Earth is _____ the Moon. (than, big)

Eng-Eng VOCA

alcohol	drinks such as beer or wine that can make people drunk
messy	dirty and untidy
light	not heavy
previous	earlier in time or order
possible	able to happen or exist; able to be done

★ 최상급을 이용한 표현

❶ 「the + 최상급」 가장 ~하다

She is the most famous photographer <u>in</u> my country. 그녀가 우리나라에서 가장 유명한 사진작가이다.

Mount Everest is the highest mountain <u>in</u> the world. 에베레스트 산이 세계에서 가장 높다.

January is the coldest month of the year <u>in</u> Korea. 한국에서는 1월이 가장 춥다.

This laptop computer is the most expensive <u>of</u> all the computers here.

이 노트북 컴퓨터가 여기에 있는 모든 컴퓨터들 중에서 가장 비싸다.

❷ 비교급과 원급을 이용한 최상급 표현

> 「**the + 최상급**」 가장 ~하다
> = 「비교급 + than any other + 단수 명사」 ~보다 더 …하다
> = 「비교급 + than all the others[other+ 복수 명사]」 다른 모든 것들보다 더 ~하다
> = 「부정어 + 비교급 + than」 ~보다 더 …한 것은 없다
> = 「부정어 + as + 원급 + as」 ~만큼 …한 것은 없다

This camera is the smallest camera in the store. 이 카메라가 가게에서 가장 작은 카메라이다.

→ This camera is smaller than any other camera in the store.

→ This is smaller than all the other cameras in the store.

→ No (other) camera in the store is smaller than this.

→ No (other) camera in the store is as small as this.

Tokyo is the largest city in Japan. 도쿄가 일본에서 가장 큰 도시이다.

→ Tokyo is larger than any other city in Japan.

→ Tokyo is larger than all the other cities in Japan.

→ No (other) city in Japan is larger than Tokyo.

→ No (other) city in Japan is as large as Tokyo.

❸ 「one of the + 최상급 + 복수 명사」 가장 ~한 것들 중 하나이다

This is one of the most luxurious rooms in this hotel. 이 방이 이 호텔에서 가장 호화로운 방 중 하나이다.

She is one of the most famous singers in the U.S.A. 그녀는 미국에ㅊㅊㅊㅊㅊ서 가장 유명한 가수 중 한 명이다.

❹ 「the + 최상급 (+ that) + 주어 + have ever p.p.」 지금까지 ~한 것 중에서 가장 ~하다

This is the most wonderful movie (that) I've ever seen.

이것이 내가 지금까지 본 것 중에서 가장 훌륭한 영화이다.

This is the most touching story (that) I've ever heard.

이것이 내가 지금까지 들은 이야기 중에서 가장 감동적인 이야기이다.

Practice

Answers p.09

A 다음 〈보기〉에서 알맞은 것을 골라 「the+최상급」을 이용하여 문장을 완성하시오.

> **plus**
> 최상급 표현에 주로 쓰이는 문장 구조
> 1)「the+최상급+in+장소나 범위의 단수 명사」
> 2)「the+최상급+of+기간·비교의 대상이 되는 복수 명사」

보기	bad	large	funny

1 My parents' room is _____ in my house.

2 John always makes us laugh. He is _____ man in my class.

3 That was _____ place I've ever been to. I will not recommend it to anyone.

B 다음 〈보기〉와 같이 문장을 완성하시오.

> **보기** The giraffe is the tallest animal in the world.
> → The giraffe is <u>taller than any other animal</u> in the world.
> → <u>No (other) animal</u> in the world is <u>taller than</u> the giraffe.
> → <u>No (other) animal</u> in the world is <u>as tall as</u> the giraffe.

1 Seoul is the most crowded city in Korea.
→ Seoul is _____ in Korea.
→ _____ in Korea is _____ Seoul.
→ _____ in Korea is _____ Seoul.

2 Michael is the fastest runner in his country.
→ Michael is _____ in his country.
→ _____ in his country is _____ Michael.
→ _____ in his country is _____ Michael.

C 다음 문장을 읽고 **틀린** 부분을 바르게 고쳐 쓰시오.

1 She is the more beautiful girl that I've ever met.

2 This house is one of the biggest house in this town.

3 No other question is most difficult than question number 17.

4 This chair is more comfortable than any other chairs in the store.

> **Eng-Eng VOCA**
> | laugh | to make sounds with your voice because you think something is funny |
> |---|---|
> | ever | at any time; at all times |
> | recommend | to say that something/someone is good |
> | crowded | too full of people or things |
> | comfortable | making you feel relaxed |

VOCA
in Grammar

Answers p.09

A 다음 주어진 단어와 비교급과 최상급을 알맞게 연결하시오.

1 well •   • a. further - furthest

2 bad •   • b. less - least

3 far •   • c. worse - worst

4 little •   • d. better - best

5 much •   • e. more - most

B 다음 괄호 안에서 알맞은 것을 고르시오.

1 My room is bigger than (my brother / my brother's).

2 This laptop computer is the most expensive (of / in) all the computers here.

3 This camera is smaller than (any / no) other camera in the store.

4 Tokyo is larger than (any / all) the other cities in Japan.

5 She is one of the most famous singers (of / in) the U.S.A.

C 다음 〈보기〉에서 알맞은 단어를 골라 문장을 완성하시오.

> **보기**   times   much   than   possible   to

1 The lake was _____ bigger than I expected.

2 My father's age is similar _____ his father's age.

3 This small wheel spins three _____ as fast as that large wheel.

4 He was probably less lucky _____ you.

5 Please give it back to me as soon as _____.

Chapter 07

가정법

Grammar
Lesson 1

★ **가정법 과거** 현재 사실에 반대되는 상황이나 실현 불가능한 일을 말할 때

> 「If+주어+동사의 과거형, 주어+조동사의 과거형+동사원형」 ~라면, ~일 텐데

If I had a cell phone, I could call him. 나에게 휴대 전화가 있다면, 그에게 전화를 걸 텐데.

→ As I don't have a cell phone, I can't call him. 나에게 휴대 전화가 없어서 그에게 전화를 걸 수 없다.

→ I don't have a cell phone, so I can't call him.

If I were free, I could go to the party. 시간이 많다면, 파티에 갈 수 있을 텐데.

→ As I'm not free, I couldn't go to the party. 시간이 없어서 파티에 갈 수 없다.

→ I'm not free, so I can't go to the party.

★ **단순 조건 vs. 가정법 과거** 실현 가능성 있음 vs. 실현 가능성 없음

If he is smart, he will solve the puzzle. (단순 조건) 만약 그가 똑똑하다면 그 퍼즐을 풀 것이다.

If he were smart, he would solve the puzzle. (가정법 조건) 그가 똑똑했더라면 그 퍼즐을 풀 텐데.

★ **가정법 과거완료** 과거 사실의 반대를 가정할 때

> 「If+주어+had+p.p. ~, 주어+조동사의 과거형+have+p.p.」 ~했다면, ~했을 텐데

If I had studied hard, I could have gotten a perfect score. 열심히 공부했다면, 나는 만점을 받았을 텐데.

→ As I didn't study hard, I couldn't get a perfect score.

If the weather had been nice yesterday, we would have gone on a picnic.
어제 날씨가 좋았다면, 소풍을 갔었을 텐데.

→ As the weather wasn't nice yesterday, we didn't go on a picnic.

★ **혼합가정법** 과거에 실현되지 못한 일이 현재에 영향을 줄 때; if절에는 과거완료를, 주절에는 과거를 씀

> 「If+주어+had+p.p., 주어+조동사의 과거형+동사원형」 ~했다면, ~할 텐데

If I had learned to swim, I could teach you how to swim now.
내가 수영을 배웠다면, 너에게 수영하는 법을 가르쳐 줄 수 있을 텐데.

→ As I didn't learn to swim, I can't teach you how to swim now.

If she had brought her smartphone, she could listen to music now.
그녀가 자신의 스마트폰을 가지고 왔다면, 지금 음악을 들을 수 있을 텐데.

→ As she didn't bring her smartphone, she can't listen to music now.

Practice

Answers p.09

A 다음 괄호 안에서 알맞은 것을 고르시오.

1 If it (isn't / weren't) raining, we could play soccer.

2 If anybody (calls / called) me, please take a message.

3 If you (throw out / threw out) the garbage, I will vacuum the carpet.

4 If the skinny jeans (aren't / weren't) too expensive, I would buy them.

5 If I (washed / had washed) my father's car, he would have raised my allowance.

B 다음 주어진 단어를 이용하여 문장을 완성하시오.

1 If she were at home, she _____ (answer) the phone.

2 If he _____ (know) the answer, he would have told me.

3 If he _____ (have) time, he would help me move the chairs.

4 If you had been more careful, you _____ (cut, not) your finger.

5 If she hadn't watched TV that late, she _____ (be, not) tired now.

C 다음 두 문장이 같은 뜻이 되도록 가정법 문장을 완성하시오.

1 As the test is not important, I won't prepare for it.

→ If the test _____ important, I _____ for it.

2 As it didn't snow a lot, we cannot make a snowman.

→ If it _____ a lot, we _____ a snowman.

3 As he was sick, he couldn't attend the meeting.

→ If he _____ sick, he _____ the meeting.

4 As I didn't save enough money, I can't buy a new car now.

→ If I _____ enough money, I _____ a new car now.

5 As she isn't good at cooking, she can't prepare food for the party by herself.

→ If she _____ good at cooking, she _____ food for the party by herself.

Eng-Eng VOCA

skinny	designed to fit closely to the body
raise	to increase an amount, number, or level
allowance	a small amount of money that a parent regularly gives to a child
careful	trying very hard to do something correctly, safely, or without causing damage
prepare (for)	to make someone/something ready for some activity

Grammar
Lesson 2

★ I wish 가정법

❶ 「I wish+과거」 ~라면 좋을 텐데 실현 불가능한 일에 대한 소망이나 현재 사실에 대한 유감을 나타낸다.

I wish I spoke Spanish fluently. 스페인어를 유창하게 한다면 좋을 텐데.
→ I'm sorry I don't speak Spanish fluently.

I wish I had a lot of money. 돈이 많으면 좋을 텐데.
→ I'm sorry I don't have a lot of money.

❷ 「I wish+과거완료」 ~했다면 좋았을 텐데 과거에 이루지 못한 일에 대한 소망이나 유감을 나타낸다.

I wish I hadn't been late for school. 학교에 지각하지 않았다면 좋았을 텐데.
→ I'm sorry that I was late for school.

I wish I had answered the question correctly. 그 질문에 제대로 대답했다면 좋았을 텐데
→ I'm sorry that I didn't answer the question correctly.

★ as if 가정법

❶ 「as if+과거」 마치 ~인 것처럼 ~하다 현재 사실에 반대되는 일을 나타낸다.

He talks as if he knew her very well. 그는 마치 그녀를 잘 아는 것처럼 말한다.
→ In fact, he doesn't know her very well.

She looks as if she were angry. 그녀는 마치 화가 난 것처럼 보인다.
→ In fact, she isn't angry.

❷ 「as if+과거완료」 마치 ~했던 것처럼 ~하다 과거 사실에 반대되는 일을 나타낸다.

He talks as if he had known her very well. 그는 마치 그녀를 잘 알았던 것처럼 말한다.
→ In fact, he didn't know her very well.

She looks as if she had been angry. 그녀는 마치 화가 났던 것처럼 보인다.
→ In fact, she wasn't angry.

★ without, but for 가정법

❶ 「without[but for]+가정법 과거」 ~이 없다면 현재 있는 것을 없다고 가정할 때 쓴다.

Without water, we could not exist. 물이 없다면, 우리는 존재할 수 없을 것이다.
→ But for water, we could not exist.
→ If it were not for water, we could not exist.

❷ 「without[but for]+가정법 과거완료」 ~이 없었다면 과거에 있던 것을 없었다고 가정할 때 쓴다.

Without your help, I wouldn't have finished the work. 너의 도움이 없었다면, 나는 그 일을 끝내지 못했을 것이다.
→ But for your help, I wouldn't have finished the work.
→ If it had not been for your help, I wouldn't have finished the work.

Practice

Answers p.10

A 다음 주어진 단어를 이용하여 문장을 완성하시오.

1 I wish my grandfather _____ (be) alive.

2 I wish I _____ (win) first prize. In fact, I lost.

3 It's too noisy here. I wish they would _____ (turn) the volume down now.

4 I wish I _____ (pay) more attention to the lecture yesterday. I don't remember anything.

5 I wish I _____ (can) buy a pair of soccer shoes.

6 We had to wait for an hour. I wish I _____ (make) a reservation.

B 다음 두 문장이 같은 뜻이 되도록 가정법 문장을 완성하시오.

1 In fact, she is embarrassed
→ She looks as if she _____ embarrassed.

2 In fact, he heard the news.
→ He acts as if he _____ the news.

3 In fact, she wasn't shocked.
→ She looks as if she _____ shocked.

4 In fact, he doesn't know the answer.
→ He acts as if he _____ the answer.

C 다음 우리말과 같은 뜻이 되도록 빈칸을 채워 문장을 완성하시오.

1 산소가 없다면, 지구상의 모든 동물은 존재하지 않을 것이다.
→ _____ oxygen, all the animals on Earth would not exist.

2 지하철이 없다면, 교통 체증이 지금보다 훨씬 심할 것이다.
→ _____ _____ the subway, the traffic would be much worse than now.

3 그의 리더십이 아니었더라면, 그들은 생존하지 못했을 것이다.
→ If it _____ _____ _____ _____ his leadership, they could not have survived.

4 컴퓨터가 없다면, 나는 내 리포트를 끝내지 못할 것이다.
→ If it _____ _____ _____ the computer, I couldn't finish my report.

Eng-Eng VOCA

alive	living; not dead
turn down	to lower the volume by moving a switch or knob
lecture	a talk that is given to teach a group of people about a subject
embarrassed	feeling confused and foolish in front of other people
act	to behave in a particular way

VOCA
in Grammar

Answers p.10

A 다음 주어진 단어가 문장의 빈칸에 알맞게 들어가도록 연결하시오.

1 would solve •

2 weren't •

3 spoke •

4 hadn't been •

5 could have gotten •

• a. If I had studied hard, I _____ a perfect score.

• b. If he were smart, he _____ the puzzle.

• c. I wish I _____ late for school.

• d. I wish I _____ Spanish fluently.

• e. If it _____ for the map, I would get lost in the woods.

B 다음 괄호 안에서 알맞은 것을 고르시오.

1 I (want / wish) I had answered the question correctly.

2 (As / As if) I don't have a cell phone, I can't call him.

3 He acts (as / because) if he knew the answer.

4 If she had been more careful, she (shouldn't / wouldn't) have hurt herself.

5 (If / When) I had learned to swim, I could teach you how to swim now.

C 다음 〈보기〉에서 알맞은 단어를 골라 문장을 완성하시오.

| 보기 | as if | but | if | without | in fact |

1 I wouldn't go to the party _____ I were you.

2 _____, he didn't know her well.

3 _____ for your help, I wouldn't have finished the work.

4 _____ water, we could not exist.

5 She looks _____ she were angry.

Chapter
08
관계사

Grammar
Lesson 1

★ 관계대명사 「접속사+대명사」의 역할

선행사	주격	목적격	소유격
사람	who	who(m)	whose
사물, 동물	which	which	whose
사람, 사물, 동물	that	that	—

* 관계대명사가 이끄는 절은 앞에 있는 명사를 수식한다. 관계대명사절의 수식을 받는 명사를 '선행사'라고 한다.

★ 주격 관계대명사 주어 역할

My father made a rocking chair. + It is in the living room.

→ My father made a rocking chair which[that] is in the living room.

우리 아버지께서 거실에 있는 흔들의자를 만드셨다.

My cousin is the same age as me. + He is coming to visit me today.

→ My cousin who[that] is coming to visit me today is the same age as me.

오늘 나를 방문할 내 사촌은 나와 나이가 같다.

★ 목적격 관계대명사 목적어 역할; 생략가능

❶ 동사의 목적어

That is the movie. + I saw the movie with my parents last Saturday.

→ That is the movie (which[that]) I saw with my parents last Saturday.

저 영화가 내가 지난 토요일에 우리 부모님과 함께 본 영화이다.

❷ 전치사의 목적어

The woman was very polite. + I spoke to her.

→ The woman (whom[that]) I spoke to was very polite.

→ The woman to whom I spoke was very polite. 나와 이야기했던 여자는 매우 예의 발랐다.

* 전치사 바로 뒤에 오는 관계대명사는 생략할 수 없고, 전치사 뒤에 that은 올 수 없다.

★ 소유격 관계대명사 소유격 역할

I met an attractive girl. + Her face was as white as snow.

→ I met an attractive girl whose face was as white as snow. 나는 얼굴이 눈처럼 하얀 매력적인 소녀를 만났다.

I had to renew books. + Their due date is coming up.

→ I had to renew books whose due date is coming up. 나는 반납일이 다가오고 있는 책의 대출 기한을 갱신해야 했다.

Practice

Answers p.11

A 다음 괄호 안에서 알맞은 것을 <u>모두</u> 고르시오.

1 The teacher (which / who / whom / that) everybody likes is absent today.

2 Rob wore a brand-new watch (which / who / whom / that) was a birthday gift from his sister.

3 I met an old friend from elementary school (which / whose / that) name I couldn't remember.

4 The music to (which / who / whom / that) we listened last night at the party was very exciting.

> **Hint**
> 관계대명사 that은 사람, 사물, 동물을 모두 선행사로 받으며, 주격과 목적격 모두에 쓸 수 있다. 단, 콤마(,)와 전치사 뒤에는 나올 수 없다.

B 다음 빈칸에 알맞은 관계대명사를 넣어 문장을 완성하시오.

1 The librarian was friendly. She showed me the books.

→ The librarian _____ showed me the books was friendly.

2 The table is a gift from my grandmother. It is in the kitchen.

→ The table _____ is in the kitchen is a gift from my grandmother.

3 She has a notebook. Its color is black.

→ She has a notebook _____ color is black.

> **Plus**
> 관계사절의 삽입으로 주어와 동사의 사이가 멀어진 경우 주어, 동사 수 일치에 주의해야 한다.
> The boys she saw on the bus are my friends.
> 그녀가 버스에서 본 소년들은 내 친구들이다.

C 다음 두 문장을 관계대명사를 이용하여 한 문장으로 만드시오.

1 He fell in love with a woman. He met her on the train.

→ He fell in love with a woman _____.

2 There are a lot of books. I have to pack them before leaving.

→ There are a lot of books _____.

3 This is the girl. We were talking about her.

→ This is the girl _____.

→ This is the girl about _____.

4 The dress was beautiful. The girl was looking at it.

→ The dress _____ at was beautiful.

→ The dress at _____ was beautiful.

> **Hint**
> 관계대명사 that은 who, whom, which로 바꿔쓸 수 있지만, whose 로 바꿔쓸 수 없다.

Eng-Eng VOCA

absent	not at work, school or a meeting because you are sick or decide not to go
librarian	a person who works in a library
friendly	kind and helpful
fall in love with	to start being in love with someone
pack	to put something into a bag or suitcase to take it with you

Grammar
Lesson 2

모바일단어장

★ 한정적 용법 vs. 계속적 용법

❶ 한정적 용법으로 쓰인 관계대명사절은 선행사를 수식하여 선행사의 의미를 한정한다.

Kelly gave me a book which [that] I've wanted to read for a long time.
Kelly가 나에게 내가 오랫동안 읽고 싶어 하던 책을 주었다.

❷ 계속적 용법으로 쓰인 관계대명사절은 선행사에 추가적인 정보를 제공하며, 보충 설명해 주는 역할을 한다.
관계대명사 that은 계속적 용법으로 쓸 수 없다.

The Eiffel Tower, which is located in Paris, was designed by Eiffel.

(→ The Eiffel Tower was designed by Eiffel, and it is located in Paris.)
에펠 탑은 Eiffel이 디자인했고, 파리에 있다.

❸ 한정적 용법과 계속적 용법의 비교

She has two daughters who are doctors. (딸이 둘 이상인 경우) 그녀는 의사인 두 딸이 있다.

She has two daughters, who are doctors. (딸이 두 명뿐인 경우) 그녀는 딸이 둘 있는데, 그들은 의사이다.

★ 관계대명사 that, what

❶ 관계대명사 that은 선행사를 포함하지 않으며, 선행사를 수식해 주는 형용사절을 이끈다.

I'll show you the skirt that I bought for her birthday. 그녀의 생일 선물로 산 치마를 보여 줄게.
(the skirt를 수식하는 형용사절)

My friend that lives in California called me yesterday. 캘리포니아에 사는 친구가 어제 나에게 전화를 했다.

❷ 관계대명사 what은 선행사를 포함하며, the thing(s) that[which]으로 바꿔 쓸 수 있다. what이 이끄는 관계대명사절은
문장에서 주어, 목적어, 보어 역할을 한다.

I'll show you what (= the thing that [which]) I bought for her birthday. 그녀의 생일 선물로 산 것을 보여 줄게.
(목적어)

What I want to know is the truth. (주어) 내가 알고 싶은 것은 진실이다.

This is what I have been looking for all day. (보어) 이것이 내가 온종일 찾던 것이다.

★ 관계대명사 that vs. 접속사 that

❶ 관계대명사 that이 관계대명사절 내에서 주어나 목적어, 보어의 역할을 하므로 관계대명사절은 주어나 목적어, 보어 중 하나가
빠진 불완전한 절이 된다.

관·대(S) V O
The man that helped us is Kevin's father. 우리를 도와준 사람은 Kevin의 아버지이다.
(주어 역할을 하는 관계대명사 that으로 뒤에 동사가 옴)

❷ 접속사 that 뒤에는 완전한 절이 온다.

접속사 S V O
I thought that she liked me. 나는 그녀가 나를 좋아한다고 생각했다.
(thought의 목적어절을 이끄는 접속사 that으로 뒤에 주어, 동사, 목적어가 있는 완전한 절이 옴)

Practice

A 다음 빈칸에 알맞은 관계대명사를 써 넣으시오.

1 I will go to see a movie with Emma, _____ is my best friend.

2 Katie, _____ is a famous British singer, will come to Korea soon.

3 Einstein, _____ received the Nobel Prize, discovered "the theory of relativity."

4 The movie, *The Terminal*, _____ was based on a true story, became very popular.

5 The Eiffel Tower, _____ is the tallest building in Paris, is one of the most popular tourist attractions in the world.

B 다음 밑줄 친 부분을 어법에 맞게 고쳐 쓰시오.

1 I don't believe <u>that</u> he told me.

2 I didn't know <u>what</u> she comes from Japan.

3 Please tell me <u>that</u> happened this morning.

4 Nancy, <u>that</u> comes from America, is outgoing.

5 This is my school, <u>that</u> is the biggest building in town.

6 <u>That</u> you just ate isn't good for you.

> **Plus**
> 계속적 용법의 관계대명사는 「접속사 +대명사」로 바꿔 쓸 수 있다.
> She has a son, <u>who</u> is a teacher.
> → She has a son <u>and he</u> is a teacher.
> 그녀는 아들이 한 명 있는데, 그는 선생님이다.

C 다음 밑줄 친 that이 관계대명사(Relative Pronoun)이면 R, 접속사(Conjunction)이면 C라고 쓰시오.

1 I heard <u>that</u> she left for Canada.

2 We heard the news <u>that</u> Rachel was elected president.

3 Cindy gave me a book <u>that</u> was very difficult to understand.

4 A zoo-keeper is a man <u>that</u> takes care of animals in a zoo.

5 Everybody likes the idea <u>that</u> we should go to a summer camp.

> **Plus**
> 동격접속사 that이 이끄는 절은 앞에 나오는 명사를 수식하고, that 뒤에는 완전한 절이 온다.
> He tried to hide <u>the fact</u> <u>that</u> he failed the exam.
> 그는 시험에 떨어졌다는 사실을 숨기려고 애썼다.

Eng-Eng VOCA

theory	an idea or set of ideas that is developed to explain facts or events
be based on	to be developed from something
attraction	an interesting or enjoyable place to go
happen	to take place especially without being planned
outgoing	liking to meet other people and being friendly towards them

Grammar
Lesson 3

관계부사는 「접속사+부사」의 역할을 하고, 앞에 나오는 선행사를 수식한다. 관계부사는 「전치사+which」로 바꿔 쓸 수 있다.

	선행사	관계부사	전치사+관계대명사
시간	the year, the time, the day	when	at/on/in+which
장소	the place, the town, the city, the house	where	at/on/in+which
이유	the reason	why	for which
방법	the way	how	in which

❶ 선행사가 시간(the year, the day, the time)인 경우, 관계부사 when을 쓴다.

I remember the day. + I first saw snow on that day.

→ I remember the day when I first saw snow.

→ I remember the day on which I first saw snow.

→ I remember the day I first saw snow. 나는 눈을 처음 본 날을 기억한다.

❷ 선행사가 장소(the place, the city, the house)인 경우, 관계부사 where를 쓴다.

This is the place. + Shakespeare was born in that place.

→ This is the place where Shakespeare was born.

→ This is the place in which Shakespeare was born.

→ This is the place (which) Shakespeare was born in. 이곳이 Shakespeare가 태어난 곳이다.

❸ 선행사가 이유(the reason)인 경우, 관계부사 why를 쓴다.

I don't know the reason. + You are angry with me for that reason.

→ I don't know the reason why you are angry with me.

→ I don't know the reason for which you are angry with me. 나는 네가 나에게 화가 난 이유를 모르겠다.

❹ 선행사가 방법(the way)인 경우, 관계부사 how를 쓴다. the way와 how는 함께 쓸 수 없다.

I'll show you the way. + You can lock the door in that way.

→ I'll show you how you can lock the door.

→ I'll show you the way you can lock the door.

→ I'll show you the way in which you can lock the door. 내가 너에게 문 잠그는 방법을 알려줄게.

   (X) I'll show you ~~the way how~~ you can lock the door.

Practice

Answers p.11

A 다음 두 문장을 관계부사(when, where, why, how)를 이용하여 한 문장으로 만드시오.

1 I don't know the way. + He got there so fast in that way.

→ I don't know _____ .

2 This is the reason. + I couldn't call you last night for that reason.

→ This is the reason _____ .

3 The town has a huge and beautiful park. + I grew up in that town.

→ The town _____ has a huge and beautiful park.

4 I remember the day. + I first went to elementary school on that day.

→ I remember the day _____ .

B 다음 〈보기〉에서 알맞은 것을 골라 문장을 완성하시오.

> Plus
> 선행사가 the time, the reason 일 때, 관계부사 또는 선행사를 생략할 수 있다. 또는 선행사를 남기고 관계부사를 생략하기도 한다.

| 보기 | the day | the hotel | the reason | the way |

1 This is _____ which we stayed at last time.

2 She explained _____ the copy machine worked.

3 I won't forget _____ when I transferred to this school.

4 I'd like to know _____ why you didn't accept my offer.

C 다음 밑줄 친 부분을 어법에 맞게 고쳐 쓰시오.

1 7 a.m. is the time <u>which</u> the mailman comes.

2 She asked me <u>the way</u> how I fixed my computer.

3 Saturday is the day <u>where</u> we played tennis together.

4 Could you explain the reason <u>how</u> you didn't wait for me?

5 A greenhouse is the building <u>which</u> you can grow plants in winter.

> **Eng-Eng VOCA**
>
> | explain | to make something clear or easy to understand |
> | work | to operate in the correct way |
> | transfer | to move from one job or school to another; to arrange for someone to move |
> | accept | to take something that someone offers you |
> | offer | something that someone says they will give you or do for you |

Grammar
Lesson 4

모바일단어장

★ 복합관계사

복합관계사는 선행사를 포함하는 관계사로 명사절과 양보의 부사절을 이끌며, 「관계사＋ever」의 형태를 취한다.

복합관계사	양보의 부사절	명사절
whoever	no matter who 누가 ~해도	anyone who ~하는 사람은 누구든지
whomever	no matter whom 누구를 ~해도	anyone whom ~하는 사람은 누구든지
whatever	no matter what 무엇을 ~해도	anything that ~하는 것은 무엇이든지

Whoever [No matter who] asks, I won't do it. 누가 부탁하더라도 나는 그것을 하지 않을 것이다.

I'll help whoever [anyone who] needs my help. 나는 나의 도움을 필요로 하는 사람은 누구든지 도와 줄 것이다.

Whomever [No matter whom] you ask, the answer will be the same. 누구에게 물어보더라도 대답은 똑같을 것이다.

You can invite whomever [anyone whom] you like. 네가 좋아하는 사람은 누구든지 초대할 수 있다.

Whatever [No matter what] you decide, I'm leaving. 네가 무슨 결정을 하더라도 나는 떠날 거야.

You may take whatever [anything that] you want. 네가 원하는 것은 무엇이든지 가져가도 좋다.

복합관계사	양보의 부사절	시간 · 장소 부사절
whenever	no matter when 언제 ~해도	at any time when [that] ~할 때면 언제나
wherever	no matter where 어디서 ~해도	at any place where [that] ~하는 곳은 어디든지
however	no matter how 아무리 ~해도	—

Whenever [No matter when] you visit us, we'll always welcome you.
네가 언제 우리를 방문하더라도 우리는 항상 너를 환영할 것이다.

Whenever [At any time when] I hear the song, it makes me think of you.
그 노래를 들을 때면 언제나 네 생각이 난다.

Wherever [No matter where] you go, you can't escape from yourself.
네가 어디를 가더라도, 너 자신에게서 도망칠 수는 없다.

You can travel wherever [at any place where] you want. 당신이 원하는 곳 어디든지 여행을 갈 수 있다.

However [No matter how] long it takes, I'll finish the project. 아무리 오래 걸리더라도 나는 그 프로젝트를 끝마칠 것이다.

Practice

Answers p.12

A 다음 밑줄 친 부분을 한 단어 바꿔 쓰시오.

1 <u>No matter who</u> asks him, he will say "No."

2 <u>At any time that</u> you want, you can go home.

3 You can sit <u>at any place that</u> you feel comfortable.

4 <u>No matter what</u> happens, I will finish my homework.

B 다음 두 문장의 의미가 같아지도록 문장을 완성하시오.

1 No matter what you do, don't be late for the meeting.

→ _____, don't be late for the meeting.

2 No matter how hard it is, you have to do it by yourself.

→ _____, you have to do it by yourself.

3 Anyone who wants to join our club, please fill in this form.

→ _____, please fill in this form.

4 On Saturdays, I usually get up at any time that I want to get up.

→ On Saturdays, I usually get up _____.

C 다음 〈보기〉에서 알맞은 것을 골라 문장을 완성하시오.

> **보기**   whenever   whatever   whoever   wherever

1 _____ calls me, tell them I'm not here.

2 I hope that you can tell me _____ is on your mind.

3 Tim is free to go anywhere he wants. He can go _____ he wants to go.

4 Evelyn is free to leave any time when she wants. She can go _____ she wants to go.

Eng-Eng VOCA

join	to become a member of an organization, society, or group
fill in	to complete a form by writing information on it
form	a document with blank spaces for filling in information
on one's mind	in one's thought; causing worry
free	able to do what you want

VOCA
in Grammar

Answers p.12

A 다음 주어진 단어에 맞도록 의미를 바르게 연결하시오.

1 whatever •   • a. at any place that

2 wherever •   • b. at any time that

3 whomever •   • c. anything that

4 however •   • d. no matter whom

5 whenever •   • e. no matter how

B 다음 괄호 안에서 알맞은 것을 고르시오.

1 I met an attractive girl (whom / whose) face was as white as snow.

2 This is the movie (which / what) I saw with my parents last Saturday.

3 She has two daughters, (who / that) are doctors.

4 I don't know the reason (for which / of which) you are angry with me.

5 (Whoever / Whomever) asks, I won't do it.

C 다음 〈보기〉에서 알맞은 단어를 골라 문장을 완성하시오.

| 보기 | where | how | what | which | that |

1 I thought _____ he liked me.

2 _____ I want to know is the truth.

3 I'll show you _____ you can lock the door.

4 This is the place _____ Shakespeare was born.

5 I remember the day on _____ I first saw snow.

Chapter

09

접속사

Grammar
Lesson 1

★ 명사절을 이끄는 접속사 that '~하는 것'

① 접속사 that이 이끄는 절은 문장에서 주어, 목적어, 보어 역할을 한다.

<u>That Michael is a very brave man</u> is totally wrong. Michael이 매우 용감한 남자라는 것은 완전히 틀렸다.
　　　　　　주어

I thought <u>(that)</u> the girl by the window was your sister. 나는 창가에 있는 소녀가 네 여동생이라고 생각했다.
　　　　　　목적어

The important fact is <u>that smoking can cause cancer.</u> 중요한 사실은 흡연이 암을 유발할 수 있다는 것이다.
　　　　　　보어

② that절이 주어로 올 때는 주어로 쓰인 that절을 문장의 뒤로 보내고 대신 그 자리에 가주어 It을 쓴다.

<u>That you follow the rules</u> is important.

→ <u>It</u> is important <u>that you follow the rules.</u> 네가 규칙을 지키는 것은 중요하다.
　가주어　　　　　　　진주어

<u>That you lost your camera</u> is unfortunate.

→ <u>It</u> is unfortunate <u>that you lost your camera.</u> 네가 카메라를 잃어버린 것은 매우 유감스러운 일이다.
　가주어　　　　　　　진주어

③ 접속사 that은 특정 명사와 함께 쓰여 동격의 명사절을 이끌기도 한다.

There is no <u>chance that he will win the competition.</u> 그가 경기에서 이길 가능성은 없다.
　　　　　└ = ┘

I was shocked to hear the <u>news that she was missing.</u> 나는 그녀가 실종되었다는 소식을 듣고 놀랐다.
　　　　　　　　　└ = ┘

★ 명사절을 이끄는 접속사 whether/if '~인지 아닌지'

<u>Whether Jacob will come (or not)</u> is not clear. Jacob이 올지 안 올지는 확실하지 않다.

The problem is <u>whether</u> we should take a taxi or a bus. 문제는 우리가 택시를 타야 하느냐 버스를 타야 하느냐이다.

I wonder <u>whether</u> she will join us (or not). 나는 그녀가 우리와 함께 할지 안 할지 궁금하다.

I don't know <u>if</u> he will visit his grandparents (or not). 나는 그가 조부모님을 방문할지 안 할지 모른다.

Practice

Answers p.12

A 다음 밑줄 친 that절의 역할을 〈보기〉에서 골라 쓰시오.

> **보기**　　　주어　　　목적어　　　보어　　　동격

1　I always think <u>that you are my best friend</u>.

2　My opinion is <u>that we should ban smoking inside buildings</u>.

3　There is a rumor <u>that you and Natalie are getting married soon</u>.

4　<u>That two different people get along with each other</u> is not true.

B 다음 주어진 문장을 〈보기〉와 같이 바꿔 쓰시오.

that절이 주어로 올 때는 주로 「It ~ that」 가주어, 진주어 구문을 이용하고, that절을 주어로 한 문장은 잘 쓰지 않는다.

> **보기**　That you have never lied to me is not true.
>
> →　　It is not true that you have never lied to me.

1　That I failed the exam is a secret.

→ _____

2　That Paul has no friends is not true.

→ _____

3　That he got a perfect score on the math exam is surprising.

→ _____

C 다음 빈칸에 if / whether / that 중 알맞은 것을 넣으시오.

① 동격절을 이끄는 접속사 that 앞에는 주로 chance, fact, idea, news, proof, rumor 등의 명사가 온다.

② or not은 주로 whether/if절의 끝에 오지만, whether 바로 뒤에 와서 whether or not으로 쓰이기도 한다.
I wonder <u>whether/if</u> he will give me a present <u>or not</u>.
= I wonder <u>whether or not</u> he will give me a present.
나는 그가 내게 선물을 줄지 안 줄지 궁금하다.

1　I want to know _____ he loves me or not.

2　I don't think _____ Mike and his brother look alike.

3　You should check _____ you turned off all the lights.

4　I'm trying to find proof _____ he stole my smartwatch.

5　She wonders _____ or not she did the interview well.

6　The news _____ he is going abroad to study makes us sad.

Eng-Eng VOCA

ban	to decide that something is not allowed
get along with	to have a friendly relationship with someone
alike	very similar
proof	facts, information, documents, etc. that prove something is true
steal	to take something from a person or store without permission

Grammar
Lesson 2

★ **의문사가 있는 간접의문문** 「의문사(접속사 역할)+주어+동사」의 어순

❶ be동사나 조동사가 있는 의문문을 간접의문문으로 만들 때는 주어 뒤에 be동사나 조동사를 그대로 쓴다.

Let me know. + What is her name?

→ Let me know what her name is. 그녀의 이름이 무엇인지 내게 알려줘.
　　　　　　　 의문사　　S　　V

Could you tell me? + Where can I get a metro map?

→ Could you tell me where I can get a metro map? 어디에서 지하철 노선도를 얻을 수 있는지 말해 주시겠어요?
　　　　　　　　　 의문사 S　V

Do you know? + When is his birthday?
→ Do you know when his birthday is? 너는 그의 생일이 언제인지 아니?

I don't know + How old is Mr. Pitt?
→ I don't know how old Mr. Pitt is. 나는 Pitt 씨가 몇 살인지 모른다.

❷ 일반동사가 있는 의문문을 간접의문문으로 만들 때는 종속절의 동사를 시제와 인칭에 알맞게 바꿔 주어야 한다.

Tell me. + When did you come home last night?

→ Tell me when you came home last night. 어젯밤에 언제 들어왔는지 내게 말해 줘.

Do you know? + What sports does Amy like?

→ Do you know what sports Amy likes? Amy가 어떤 운동을 좋아하는지 아니?

★ **의문사가 없는 간접의문문** 「접속사(whether/if)+주어+동사」의 어순; '~인지 아닌지'

I wonder. + Could you help me?
→ I wonder whether[if] you could help me. 나는 네가 나를 도와줄 수 있는지 궁금하다.
　　　　　 접속사　S　　V

Can you tell me? + Did Sally lie to me?
→ Can you tell me whether[if] Sally lied to me? Sally가 나에게 거짓말을 했는지 안 했는지 내게 말해 줄 수 있니?
　　　　　　　　　 접속사　　S　　V

72

Practice

Answers p.13

A 다음 두 문장을 한 문장의 간접의문문으로 바꿔 쓰시오.

1 I have no idea. + Where is Tom now?

→ I have no idea _____ .

2 Do you know? + What does Mary's younger sister do?

→ Do you know _____ ?

3 Could you tell me? + When did you see Sally?

→ Could you tell me _____ ?

B 다음 두 문장을 한 문장의 간접의문문으로 바꿔 쓰시오.

1 Please tell me. + What made you cry?

→ _____

2 I wonder. + Where did he go last Saturday?

→ _____

3 I don't know. + When will she come home?

→ _____

C 다음 〈보기〉와 같이 간접의문문 문장을 완성하시오.

보기 Have you seen Tom lately?

→ I wonder _____ whether[if] you have seen Tom lately _____ .

1 Is Susan a veterinarian?

→ I don't know _____ .

2 Did you do your homework?

→ Tell me _____ .

3 Have you ever been to Paris?

→ I'm wondering _____ .

4 Are we going out for dinner?

→ Do you know _____ ?

Eng-Eng VOCA

idea	an understanding of something; knowledge about something
know	to have some information in your mind
wonder	to have interest in learning something
lately	in a recent period of time
veterinarian	a person who gives medical care and treatment to animals

Grammar
Lesson 3

❶ 시간을 나타내는 접속사

When[As] Ben first came to Korea, he couldn't speak Korean at all.   Ben은 한국에 처음 왔을 때 한국어를 전혀 못 했다.

I got home while my mother was washing the dishes.   나는 엄마가 설거지를 할 때 집에 도착했다.

He finished his homework before he had dinner.   그는 저녁을 먹기 전에 숙제를 끝냈다.

Eva will take a long vacation after she finishes this project.   Eva는 이 프로젝트를 끝낸 후에 긴 휴식을 취할 것이다.

Leo has met a lot of good people since he went to college.   Leo는 대학에 들어온 이래로 좋은 사람들을 많이 만났다.

I took a nap until my roommate Mona woke me up.   나는 룸메이트 Mona가 깨울 때까지 낮잠을 잤다.

* 시간을 나타내는 접속사로는 when, as(~할 때), while(~하는 동안, ~하던 중에), before(~하기 전에),
  after(~한 후에), since(~한 이래로), until(~할 때까지) 등이 있다.

❷ 조건을 나타내는 접속사

You can visit me anytime you want if you need my advice.   내 조언이 필요하다면 언제든지 나를 방문해도 된다.

Unless you like sports, you can change the channel.   네가 스포츠를 좋아하지 않으면 채널을 돌려도 된다.
→ If you don't like sports, you can change the channel.

* 조건을 나타내는 접속사로는 if(만약 ~한다면), unless(만약 ~하지 않으면) 등이 있다.

❸ if 조건문의 명령문 전환

If you get up early, you can have breakfast before you go to school.   일찍 일어나면, 등교하기 전에 아침을 먹을 수 있다.
→ Get up early, and you can have breakfast before you go to school.

Unless you work out regularly, you'll gain weight.   규칙적으로 운동을 하지 않으면 살이 찔 것이다.
→ Work out regularly, or you'll gain weight.

*if 조건문은 「명령문, and ~」로 바꿔 쓸 수 있고, unless[if … not] 조건문은 「명령문, or ~」로 바꿔 쓸 수 있다.

❹ 시간, 조건을 나타내는 부사절의 시제

I will call you when I arrive at the airport. (O)   내가 공항에 도착하면 네게 전화할게.

I will call you when I will arrive at the airport. (X)

If it rains tomorrow, I will give you a ride. (O)   내일 비가 오면 차로 데려다 줄게.

If it will rain tomorrow, I will give you a ride. (X)

* 시간이나 조건을 나타내는 부사절에서는 현재시제가 미래시제를 대신한다.

Practice

Answers p.13

A 다음 괄호 안에서 알맞은 것을 고르시오.

1 Don't open your eyes (since / until) I count to ten.

2 (When / If) I looked up in the sky, there was a rainbow.

3 She called me three times (before / while) I was taking a shower.

4 I haven't met Jason (since / when) he went abroad to study English.

5 (If / Unless) it rains, I will stay home tomorrow.

6 (Since / Because of) you are smarter than me, why don't you teach her?

> **Plus**
>
> 접속사 when은 '~할 때'의 뜻으로 「when+주어+동사」의 어순으로 쓰고, 의문사 when은 '언제'라는 뜻으로 「when+동사+주어 ~?」의 어순으로 쓴다.
>
> (접속사)
> When you are at home, what do you usually do?
> 너는 집에 있을 때 주로 무엇을 하니?
>
> (의문사)
> When are you at home?
> 너는 언제 집에 있니?

B 다음 〈보기〉에서 알맞은 것을 골라 문장을 완성하시오.

보기   if   unless   and   or

1 Let's go there on foot _____ it snows heavily.

2 _____ you're not busy, could you give me a hand?

3 Stop eating at night, _____ you will gain a lot of weight.

4 Be honest all the time, _____ people around you will trust you.

C 다음 우리말과 같은 뜻이 되도록 빈칸에 알맞은 접속사를 쓰시오.

1 내가 백화점에 갔을 때 백화점은 이미 문을 닫았다.

→ _____ I went to the department store, it was closed already.

2 나는 중국을 방문하기 전에 중국에 관한 책 몇 권을 읽었다.

→ I had read some books about China _____ I visited China.

3 나와도 괜찮을 때까지 네 방에 있어라.

→ Stay in your room _____ it is okay to come out.

4 만약 내가 표를 살 만한 여유가 있다면 비행기를 타고 하와이에 갈 것이다.

→ I'll go to Hawaii by plane _____ I can afford to buy a ticket.

Eng-Eng VOCA

on foot	by walking
give ~ a hand	to help someone
all the time	always; very often
trust	to believe that someone is good, sincere, and honest
afford	to be able to pay for something

Grammar
Lesson 4

★ 부사절을 이끄는 접속사 II 〈이유, 양보〉

❶ 이유를 나타내는 접속사

I was very angry **because** my nephew dropped my cell phone, and it was broken.
나는 조카가 내 휴대전화를 떨어트려서 그것이 고장 났기 때문에 매우 화가 났다.

Since you will leave earlier than me, give the key to me. 너는 나보다 더 일찍 떠날 거니까 내게 열쇠를 줘.

As it is getting dark, I should go home. 날이 점점 어두워지니까 나는 집에 가야 한다.

The fans are leaving the concert hall **now (that)** the concert is over. 콘서트가 끝나서 팬들이 콘서트장을 떠나고 있다.

* 이유를 나타내는 접속사는 because, since, as, now (that) 등이 있고, '~ 때문에', '~여서', '~이니까' 등으로 해석한다.

▷ 접속사 because vs. 전치사 because of

접속사 because 뒤에는 절(주어+동사)이 오고, 전치사 because of 뒤에는 명사(구)가 온다.

It is cold today **because** <u>it snowed</u> last night. 어젯밤에 내린 눈 때문에 오늘은 춥다.
　　　　　　　　　　　　절 (S + V)

→ It is cold today **because of** <u>the snow</u> of last night.
　　　　　　　　　　　　　　　명사(구)

We couldn't go on a field trip **because** <u>it was raining</u>.
　　　　　　　　　　　　　　　　절 (S + V)

→ We couldn't go on a field trip **because of** <u>rain</u>. 비 때문에 현장학습을 가지 못했다.
　　　　　　　　　　　　　　　　명사

❷ 양보를 나타내는 접속사

I couldn't get any sleep, **though** I was very exhausted. 나는 매우 피곤했음에도 불구하고 잠들 수 없었다.

Although you are my best friend, I can't help you this time.
비록 너는 나의 가장 친한 친구이지만 이번에는 너를 도와줄 수 없어.

I don't speak Japanese, **even though** I have been living in Tokyo for five years.
나는 도쿄에서 5년 동안 살고 있지만, 일본어를 할 줄 모른다.

* 양보를 나타내는 접속사는 though, although, even though 등이 있고, '비록 ~일지라도', '~에도 불구하고' 등으로 해석한다.

▷ 접속사 although [(even) though] vs. 전치사 despite [in spite of]

양보의 뜻을 가진 전치사에는 despite, in spite of 등이 있고 '~에도 불구하고'라고 해석한다.
접속사 뒤에는 절이 오고, 전치사의 뒤에는 명사(구)가 온다.

Mina and I went shopping, **although** <u>it snowed heavily</u>. Mina와 나는 눈이 매우 많이 내렸지만 쇼핑을 갔다.
　　　　　　　　　　　　　　　　　절 (S + V)

→ Mina and I went shopping **despite** <u>the heavy snow</u>.
　　　　　　　　　　　　　　　　　명사(구)

I got there in time, **even though** <u>I got up late this morning</u>. 나는 오늘 아침에 늦게 일어났지만, 제시간에 그곳에 도착했다.
　　　　　　　　　　　　　　　절 (S + V)

→ I got there in time **in spite of** <u>getting up late this morning</u>.
　　　　　　　　　　　　　　　　　명사(구)

Practice

Answers p.13

A 다음 두 문장이 같은 뜻이 되도록 빈칸에 알맞은 말을 쓰시오.

1 The school bus was on time in spite of the traffic jam.

= The school bus was on time _____ there was a traffic jam.

2 The field trip was canceled because the weather was terrible.

= The field trip was canceled _____ the terrible weather.

3 She decided not to accept the job because of the low salary.

= She decided not to accept the job _____ the salary was low.

4 Even though she invited me, I didn't go to her birthday party.

= _____ her invitation, I didn't go to her birthday party.

B 다음 〈보기〉에서 알맞은 것을 골라 문장을 완성하시오.

> **보기**   because   because of   even though   in spite of

1 _____ getting up early, I was late for school.

2 I was late for school _____ my laziness.

3 James failed the exam _____ he didn't study at all.

4 James failed the exam _____ he studied very hard.

C 다음 우리말과 같은 뜻이 되도록 문장을 완성하시오.

1 나는 소음 때문에 일에 집중할 수 없었다.

→ I couldn't concentrate on my work _____ the noise.

2 날씨가 점점 추워지니까 새 스웨터를 하나 사야겠다.

→ _____ it is getting cold, I should buy a new sweater.

3 이 건물은 지진에도 불구하고 전혀 피해를 입지 않았다.

→ This building was not damaged at all _____ the earthquake.

Eng-Eng VOCA

field trip	a visit to a place made by students to learn about something
salary	money that employees receive for doing their job
concentrate on	to give all your attention to something
damage	to harm or spoil something
earthquake	a sudden shaking of the Earth's surface

VOCA in Grammar

Answers p.14

A 다음 주어진 단어가 문장의 빈칸에 알맞게 들어가도록 연결하시오.

1 if •   • a. Let me know _____ her name is.

2 where •   • b. I don't know _____ old Mr. Pitt is.

3 what •   • c. Do you know _____ his birthday is?

4 when •   • d. Can you tell me _____ Sally lies to me?

5 how •   • e. Could you tell me _____ I can get a metro map?

B 다음 괄호 안에서 알맞은 것을 고르시오.

1 It is unfortunate (what / that) you lost your camera.

2 We couldn't go on a field trip (because / because of) it was raining.

3 (Despite / Although) you are my best friend, I can't help you this time.

4 I wonder (whether / that) you could help me.

5 I took a nap (as / until) my roommate Mona woke me up.

C 다음 〈보기〉에서 알맞은 단어를 골라 문장을 완성하시오.

> 보기   and   or   while   unless   since

1 Leo has met a lot of good people _____ he went to college.

2 Work out regularly, _____ you'll gain weight.

3 _____ you like sports, you can change the channel.

4 Get up early, _____ you can have breakfast before you go to school.

5 I got home _____ my mother was washing the dishes.

Chapter
10
화법, 강조, 도치, 일치

Grammar
Lesson 1

★ 화법

❶ 직접화법 큰따옴표를 이용해서 다른 사람의 말을 그대로 전달하는 방식

Sean says, "I'm thirsty." Sean이 "나 목말라."라고 말한다.

Rachel said, "I have to leave." Rachel이 "나는 가야 해."라고 말했다.

❷ 간접화법 다른 사람이 말한 내용을 전달하는 사람의 입장에서 바꿔 말하는 방식

Sean says that he is thirsty. Sean이 목이 마르다고 말한다.

Rachel said that she had to leave. Rachel이 떠나야 한다고 말했다.

★ 평서문의 화법 전환

Greg said, "I am going to school now."
→ Greg said (that) he was going to school then. Greg는 그때 학교에 가고 있는 중이라고 말했다.

① 전달 동사를 쓴다. said → said, said to → said to 또는 told

② 쉼표(,)와 큰따옴표(" ")를 삭제하고, 접속사 that을 쓴다. 이때 접속사 that은 생략 가능하다.

③ that절의 주어와 목적어 등을 적절하게 바꾼다.

④ that절의 시제를 주절의 시제를 고려하여 적절하게 바꾼다. 전달 동사가 현재 → 현재로, 과거 → 과거나 과거완료로 쓴다.

⑤ that절의 부사를 적절하게 바꾼다.

★ 화법 전환 시의 시제 변화: 현재 → 현재, 과거 → 과거 또는 과거완료

Kevin says, "I am so happy to see you." (전달동사가 현재 → that절 동사는 현재)

→ Kevin says that he is so happy to see me. Kevin은 나를 만나서 기쁘다고 말한다.

Kevin said, "I am so happy to see you." (전달동사가 과거 → that절 동사는 과거)

→ Kevin said that he was so happy to see me. Kevin은 나를 만나서 기뻤다고 말했다.

Kevin said, "I wanted to see you." (전달동사가 과거 → that절 동사는 과거완료)

→ Kevin said that he had wanted to see me. Kevin은 나를 보고 싶었다고 말했다.

▷ 화법 전환 시의 부사구의 변화

직접화법	간접화법	직접화법	간접화법
this	that	last	the previous
these	those	next	the following
here	there	today	that day
ago	before	yesterday	the day before, the previous day
now	then	tomorrow	the next day, the following day

Practice

Answers p.14

A 다음 두 문장이 같은 뜻이 되도록 괄호 안에서 알맞은 것을 고르시오.

1 Tim said to me, "I'll play soccer tomorrow."

→ Tim told me that he (will / would) play soccer the following day.

2 Cindy said, "I'm visiting Jeju next month."

→ Cindy said that she (is / was) visiting Jeju the following month.

3 Brian said to me, "I have already finished washing the dishes."

→ Brian told me that he (has / had) already finished washing the dishes.

B 다음 문장을 간접화법 문장으로 바꿀 때, 밑줄 친 부분을 바르게 고쳐 쓰시오.

1 Daniel said to me, "I have to prepare for the interview."

→ Daniel told me that I had to prepare for the interview.

2 Ally said to me, "I will hang out in the park after school."

→ Ally told me that she will hang out in the park after school.

3 Michael said to me, "I can teach you how to swim."

→ Michael told me that he could teach you how to swim.

4 Catherine said to me, "I have a doctor's appointment tomorrow."

→ Catherine told me that she has a doctor's appointment the next day.

C 다음 두 문장이 같은 뜻이 되도록 간접화법 문장을 완성하시오.

1 Sally said, "I will study in the library this Sunday."

→ Sally said that _____.

2 Mom said, "You can watch TV after you finish your homework."

→ Mom said that _____.

3 Peter said, "I came to London last year."

→ Peter said that _____.

4 George said to me, "I haven't heard from Brian since last month."

→ George told me that _____.

following	coming next; listed or shown next
interview	a meeting at which someone is asked questions to see if they are suitable for a position
appointment	an arrangement for meeting at an agreed time and place, for a particular purpose
library	a building containing books that can be borrowed
hear from	to receive a letter or phone call from someone

Grammar
Lesson 2

★ 의문사가 있는 의문문의 화법 전환

She said to me, " What do you want for dessert?"

  ①   ②

→ She asked me what I wanted for dessert. 그녀는 나에게 디저트로 무엇을 원하냐고 물었다.

 ① 전달동사를 ask 등으로 바꾼다.

 ② 의문문을 「의문사＋주어＋동사 ～」의 어순으로 쓰면서, 주어와 동사, 부사 등을 문맥에 맞게 바꿔 준다.

Amy said to me, "Who bought you the coat?"

→ Amy asked me who had bought me the coat. Amy는 나에게 누가 그 코트를 사줬냐고 물었다.

Jason said to me, "Where are you going?"

→ Jason asked me where I was going. Jason은 나에게 어디에 가고 있느냐고 물었다.

★ 의문사가 없는 의문문의 화법 전환

He said to me, "Do you want to see a movie today?"

  ①   ②

→ He asked me if [whether] I wanted to see a movie that day. 그는 그날 영화 보러 가기를 원하느냐고 물었다.

 ① 전달동사를 ask 등으로 바꾼다.

 ② 의문문을 「whether / if ＋주어＋동사」의 어순으로 쓰면서, 주어와 동사, 부사 등을 문맥에 맞게 바꿔 준다.

He said to me, "Did she bring her cell phone?"

→ He asked me whether [if] she had brought her cell phone. 그는 나에게 그녀가 휴대 전화를 가져왔는지 물었다.

Terry said to me, "Will she come to the party?"

→ Terry asked me whether [if] she would come to the party. Terry가 나에게 그녀가 파티에 올 것인지 물었다.

★ 명령문의 화법 전환

He said to me, "Wait for me."

→ He told me to wait for him. 그는 나에게 기다려 달라고 말했다.

She said to them, "Don't worry."

→ She told them not to worry. 그녀는 그들에게 걱정하지 말라고 말했다.

 ① 전달동사를 tell, ask, advise, order 등으로 문맥에 맞게 바꿔 준다.

 ② 명령문의 동사 앞에 to를 붙인다. 단, 부정 명령문은 not to를 붙인다.

Practice

Answers p.14

A 다음 두 문장이 같은 뜻이 되도록 간접화법 문장을 완성하시오.

1 Emma said to me, "Where are you going?"

→ Emma asked me _____.

2 Fred said to me, "Why were you late?"

→ Fred asked me _____.

3 Harry said to me, "What subject do you like the most?"

→ Harry asked me _____.

B 다음 두 문장이 같은 뜻이 되도록 간접화법 문장을 완성하시오.

1 Kimberly said to me, "Can I borrow your pencil?"

→ Kimberly asked me _____.

2 Ben said to me, "Have you seen my notebook?"

→ Ben asked me _____.

3 Amanda said to me, "Do you want something to drink?"

→ Amanda asked me _____.

4 Emily said to me, "Are you coming to the housewarming party?"

→ Emily asked me _____.

C 다음 문장을 간접화법 문장으로 바꿀 때, 밑줄 친 부분을 바르게 고쳐 쓰시오.

1 James said to me, "Drive carefully."

→ James advised me <u>drive</u> carefully.

2 Chris said to me, "Be quiet."

→ Chris told me <u>if I</u> be quiet.

3 My mother said to me, "Don't stay up too late."

→ My mother told me <u>don't</u> stay up too late.

4 Ian said to me, "Do not take the subway."

→ Ian advised me <u>no</u> take the subway.

Eng-Eng VOCA

subject	an area of knowledge that is studied in school
borrow	to take something with the promise of returning it at a later time
housewarming party	a party to celebrate someone's move to a new home
stay up	to not go to bed at the time you would normally do so
advise	to tell someone what they should do

Grammar
Lesson 3

★ 강조

❶ 동사를 강조할 때는 「do/does/did＋동사원형」의 형태로 쓰고, '정말 ～하다'라고 해석한다.

Edward does look exhausted. Edward는 정말 피곤해 보인다.

I did wait for you there for almost one hour. 나는 정말 너를 거기서 한 시간이나 기다렸다.

❷ 주어, 목적어, 부사 등을 강조할 때는 「It ～ that」 구문을 이용한다.

강조하고자 하는 말을 that 앞에 두고 '～한 것은 바로 ～였다'라고 해석한다.

Bella ran into Edward in the park last Saturday.
Bella는 지난 토요일에 공원에서 Edward와 우연히 마주쳤다.

It was Bella that[who] ran into Edward in the park last Saturday.
지난 토요일에 공원에서 Edward를 우연히 마주친 사람은 바로 Bella였다.

It was Edward that[who(m)] Bella ran into in the park last Saturday.
Bella가 지난 토요일에 공원에서 우연히 마주친 사람은 바로 Edward였다.

It was in the park that[where] Bella ran into Edward last Saturday.
Bella가 지난 토요일에 Edward와 우연히 마주친 곳은 바로 공원이었다.

It was last Saturday that[when] Bella ran into Edward in the park.
Bella가 공원에서 Edward를 우연히 마주친 날은 바로 지난 토요일이었다.

★ 도치 주어＋동사 → 동사＋주어로 어순이 바뀜

❶ 부사구나 부정어를 강조하는 도치문

Under the bed were several pairs of socks. 여러 켤레의 양말이 침대 밑에 있었다.

← Several pairs of socks were under the bed.

Hardly does she make a mistake. 그녀는 거의 실수를 하지 않는다.

← She hardly makes a mistake.

Never have I seen such a beautiful garden. 나는 한 번도 이렇게 아름다운 정원을 본 적이 없다.

← I have never seen such a beautiful garden.

Here comes my mother. 여기 우리 엄마가 오신다.

There goes my English teacher. 저기 우리 선생님이 지나가신다.

❷ so, neither, nor의 도치문 동사가 주어보다 먼저 온다.

A: I'm so hungry. I want to eat something. 나는 배가 많이 고파. 뭔가를 좀 먹어야겠어.

B: So do I. 나도 그래.

A: It's cold outside. I'm not going out tonight. 밖이 추워. 오늘 밤에는 나가지 않을 거야.

B: Neither am I. 나도 그래.

A: Did you and your sister finish cleaning the rooms? 너와 네 동생은 방 청소를 다 했니?

B: No. I didn't clean my room, nor did my sister. 아니. 나도 안 했고, 내 동생도 안 했어.

Practice

Answers p.15

A 다음 밑줄 친 부분을 강조하는 문장으로 바꿔 쓰시오.

Hint
강조하는 대상에 따라 that 대신 who(m), when, where 등을 쓸 수 있다.

1 I believe what he told me.

→ I _____ believe what he told me.

2 She is a good singer. She sings very well.

→ She is a good singer. She _____ sing very well.

3 The man that stepped on my foot apologized to me.

→ The man that stepped on my foot _____ apologize to me.

4 Justin asked Sarah out last night.

→ It was _____ Justin asked Sarah out.

5 Anna studied English Literature in London last year.

→ It was _____ Anna studied English Literature last year.

B 다음 밑줄 친 부분을 강조하는 문장으로 바꿔 쓰시오.

1 She would never do anything to harm you.

→ Never _____ anything to harm you.

2 An old castle stood on the hill.

→ On the hill _____ an old castle.

3 He hardly helps me do the household chores.

→ Hardly _____ me do the household chores.

C 다음 빈칸에 알맞은 대답을 써 넣어 대화를 완성하시오.

1 A: I don't regret what I did.

B: Neither _____. We did the right thing.

2 A: I'm terribly cold.

B: So _____. Today, the temperature dropped below zero.

3 A: Can you and your brother speak Spanish?

B: I can't speak Spanish, nor _____. We only speak English.

Eng-Eng VOCA

step on	to put your foot on something
ask ~ out	to ask someone to go on a date with you
household chore	a small job that you do regularly to keep a house clean
regret	to feel sorry about something you did or did not do
temperature	a measurement that shows how hot or cold something is

Grammar
Lesson 4

★ 시제 일치 주절의 시제 = 종속절의 시제

I don't think that he came to the party last night. 내 생각에 그는 지난밤 파티에 오지 않았던 것 같다.
We believe that you'll succeed. 우리는 네가 성공할 거라고 믿는다.
I thought that I heard something. 나는 무슨 소리를 들었다고 생각했다.
She realized that she had been here before. 그녀는 전에 여기에 와본 적이 있다는 것을 깨달았다.

* 주절이 현재이면 종속절에 거의 모든 시제를 쓸 수 있지만, 주절이 과거이면 종속절에 주로 과거나 과거완료가 온다.

★ 시제 일치의 예외

I learned that light travels faster than sound. 나는 빛이 소리보다 빠르다는 것을 배웠다.
I know that Alfred Nobel invented dynamite. 나는 Alfred Nobel이 다이너마이트를 발명했다는 것을 안다.

*일반적인 진리나 현재의 습관 등 현재에도 사실인 것은 주로 현재로, 역사적 사실은 과거로 쓴다.

★ 수의 일치

❶ 상관접속사

both A and B +복수동사	Both my sister and I like to travel to other countries. 나와 내 여동생은 다른 나라를 여행하는 것을 좋아한다.
either A or B: B에 수 일치	Either you or he has to clean up this mess. 너나 그 중에 한 사람이 이 어질러진 것을 치워야 한다.
not only A but also B = B as well as A: B에 수 일치	Not only my sisters but also I am going to visit you tonight. → I as well as my sisters am going to visit you tonight. 우리 부모님뿐만 아니라 나도 이번 주말에 너를 방문할 것이다.

❷ 주의해야 할 단·복수 표현

학문명, 병명 등	I don't think that economics is a difficult subject. 나는 경제학이 어려운 과목이라고 생각하지 않는다.
거리, 시간, 무게, 금액 등의 단위	Two kilometers is not that far to walk. 2km는 걷기에 그렇게 멀지는 않다.
each, every, -thing, -one, -body	Every student has his or her own computer. 모든 학생은 개인 컴퓨터를 가지고 있다. Each nation has its own national anthem. 나라마다 국가가 있다.
the number of +복수 명사+단수 동사	The number of high school students in town has increased sharply. 마을의 고등학생 수가 급격하게 증가했다.
a number of +복수 명사+복수 동사	A number of students were standing in the playground. 많은 학생들이 운동장에 서 있었다.

❸ 삽입구(절)로 주어와 동사의 사이가 멀어진 경우의 수 일치

The girl who is wearing jeans is 16 years old. 청바지를 입고 있는 소녀는 열여섯 살이다.
Eating many candies is not good for your teeth. 사탕을 많이 먹는 것은 치아에 좋지 않다.
People living in Florida like water sports. 플로리다에 사는 사람들은 해상스포츠를 좋아한다.

Practice

Answers p.15

A 다음 괄호 안에서 알맞은 것을 고르시오.

1 She believed that he (will / would) keep his promise.

2 I know that the Berlin Wall (is / was) torn down in 1989.

3 He thought that he (hear / heard) somebody screaming.

4 We learned that the Earth (circles / circled) around the Sun.

5 My friends didn't think Clara (can / could) speak Korean, but her
Korean is actually great.

B 다음 밑줄 친 부분을 어법에 맞게 고쳐 쓰시오.

1 James believed that he <u>sees</u> Kelly here earlier.

2 The girl told me that she <u>bit</u> her nails when she feels nervous.

3 We all knew the fact that a triangle <u>had</u> three sides.

4 The teacher said that she <u>is</u> very happy to meet us yesterday.

5 Mr. Sanders taught us that water <u>boiled</u> at 100℃.

6 Patrick told us that his children <u>are</u> born in 2005.

C 다음 주어진 단어를 이용하여 문장을 완성하시오.

1 Rachel's sisters as well as Rachel _____ (live) in New York City.

2 Either my brother or I _____ (have) to take care of my baby brother.

3 Not only Nancy but also her parents _____ (be) not home when I got there.

4 Thirty minutes _____ (be) not enough time to get to the airport.

5 A large number of people _____ (be) gathering into the town square now.

6 My grandmother who lives in the countryside _____ (grow) vegetables and flowers.

Eng-Eng VOCA

tear down	to destroy a building deliberately
nervous	worried or frightened about something, and unable to relax
gather	to come together and form a group
square	an open area in a town, surrounded by buildings
grow	to make plants or crops develop and produce fruit or flowers

VOCA
in Grammar

Answers p.15

A 다음 대화가 자연스럽도록 알맞게 연결하시오.

    A   *B*

1 I'm so hungry.   •   • a. Neither did I.

2 I like English best.   •   • b. Neither am I.

3 I didn't watch that movie.   •   • c. So am I.

4 I have been to China before.   •   • d. So do I.

5 I'm not going out tonight.   •   • e. So have I.

B 다음 괄호 안에서 알맞은 것을 고르시오.

1 (A number of / The number of) high school students in town has increased sharply.

2 I don't think that (economic / economics) is a difficult subject.

3 I didn't clean my room, (or / nor) did my sister.

4 (Hard / Hardly) does she make a mistake.

5 It was in the park (when / where) Bella ran into Edward last Saturday.

C 다음 〈보기〉에서 알맞은 단어를 골라 문장을 완성하시오.

> **보기**   as well as   both   either   not only   each

1 _____ student has his or her own computer.

2 _____ you or he has to clean up this mess.

3 James _____ his parents is excited about their trip.

4 _____ my brothers but also I am going to visit you tonight.

5 _____ my sister and I like to travel to other countries.

A 다음 문장을 「It ~ to …」 문장으로 바꿔 쓰시오.

1 To learn French is very difficult.

→ _____

2 To swim in the sea is dangerous.

→ _____

3 To complete the project alone was impossible.

→ _____

4 To play soccer in the rain can be fun.

→ _____

B 다음 밑줄 친 부분을 어법에 맞게 고쳐 문장을 다시 쓰시오.

1 It's to go time to bed.

→ _____

2 Can I have to drink something?

→ _____

3 Andy doesn't have many friends to play.

→ _____

4 The students need some paper to write.

→ _____

C 다음 우리말과 같은 뜻이 되도록 주어진 단어를 배열하시오.

1 나의 고양이는 20살까지 살았다. (20 years old, to be, my cat, lived)

→ _____

2 우리에게 진실을 말해주다니 너는 무척 용감하구나. (to tell us, very brave, was, the truth, of, it, you)

→ _____

3 우리는 더 똑똑해지기 위해 많은 책을 읽어야 한다. (many books, we, smarter, read, to become, should)

→ _____

4 너의 어머니는 그곳에서 나를 만나서 매우 기뻐하셨다. (to see, your mother, there, was, me, so happy)

→ _____

5 이 퍼즐은 풀기에 정말 쉽다. (really easy, is, this puzzle, to solve)

→ _____

A 다음 주어진 단어를 이용하여 빈칸에 알맞은 의미상 주어를 써넣으시오.

1 The poem is too difficult _____ to understand. (I)

2 It is impolite _____ to talk back to your teacher like that. (you)

3 It wasn't easy _____ to move all the boxes into the building. (they)

4 It is very sweet _____ to write a song for me. (he)

5 It was really generous _____ to make the donation. (she)

6 It isn't possible _____ to get to the station in time. (we)

B 다음 밑줄 친 부분을 어법에 맞게 고쳐 쓰시오.

1 It's very rude <u>for you</u> to say so.　　　　　　　→ _____

2 He is very happy <u>to invite</u> to your party.　　　→ _____

3 I want this shirt <u>to wash</u> right now.　　　　　→ _____

4 It was very foolish <u>for him</u> to make his sister cry.　→ _____

5 They seem <u>that they know</u> where I live.　　　→ _____

6 She didn't bring her purse. She seems <u>to lose</u> it.　→ _____

C 다음 빈칸에 주어진 단어의 알맞은 형태를 써 대화문을 완성하시오.

Shawn: Oh, no. The computer is not working again.

Kate:　What did you do?

Shawn: I don't know. I seem to ⓐ _____ (open) too many programs at the same time, but I am not sure.

Kate:　You should call James if you want it to ⓑ _____ (repair).

Shawn: James?

Kate:　Yeah. He's a computer genius. It won't be hard ⓒ _____ (he) to fix the computer.

Shawn: Okay. I will call him right now.

ⓐ _____　　　ⓑ _____　　　ⓒ _____

A 다음 보기에서 알맞은 단어를 골라 어법에 맞게 바꿔 문장을 완성하시오.

> **보기**   smoke   call   join   speak   accept   eat

1 You need to avoid _____ too much meat.

2 Remember _____ me right after you arrive at the airport.

3 He finally agreed _____ their offer.

4 My sister decided _____ the army.

5 If you want to improve your English, try _____ as much as possible.

6 I really want my father to quit _____ for his health.

B 다음 문장을 읽고 어법상 어색한 부분을 찾아 바르게 고치시오.

1 Mrs. Clark is planning visit the museum with us next week.

_____ → _____

2 The scientist finished to do experiments with the bacteria.

_____ → _____

3 It is hard to imagine to live alone on this island.

_____ → _____

4 I didn't expect see you here.

_____ → _____

C 다음 우리말과 같은 뜻이 되도록 주어진 단어를 이용하여 문장을 완성하시오.

1 나는 바닥에 있는 동전을 주우려고 멈췄다. (stop, pick up)

→ I _____ the coin on the floor.

2 그는 어제 나와 농구한 것이 기억나지 않는다. (remember, play)

→ He doesn't _____ basketball with me yesterday.

3 나의 형은 액션 영화 보는 것을 즐긴다. (enjoy, watch)

→ My brother _____ action movies.

4 나갈 때 문 잠그는 것을 제발 잊지 마. (forget, lock)

→ Please, don't _____ the door when you leave.

A 다음 〈보기〉에서 단어를 골라 알맞은 형태로 바꿔 문장을 완성하시오.

> **보기**   come   solve   go   cry

1 I heard some children _____ last night.

2 My teacher made me _____ a lot of math problems.

3 Please let me _____ to the dance party.

4 The boss told me _____ to work earlier.

B 다음 우리말과 같은 뜻이 되도록 주어진 단어를 이용하여 문장을 완성하시오.

1 너는 그 방에 들어가면 안 돼. (supposed, enter)

   → You _____ the room.

2 나는 너무 놀라서 그녀에게 인사할 수 없었다.

   → I was _____ hi to her. (surprised, say)

3 사실을 말하자면, 나는 그녀와 사랑에 빠졌다. (tell, truth)

   → _____, I am in love with her.

4 그들은 나를 그들에 파티에 초대할 만큼 친절했다. (kind, invite)

   → They were _____ me to their party.

C 다음 대화문을 읽고 물음에 답하시오.

> **Will:**   I stayed up until 3 a.m. ⓐ <u>I am too tired to study now.</u>
>
> **Mike:** You should always go to bed early to get enough sleep.
>
> **Will:**   I know, but I couldn't help it. My favorite singer was on TV last night.
>
> **Mike:** Look at you now. You look very tired, and it seems that you can't even open your eyes. ⓑ <u>너의 부모님께서는 네가 TV를 많이 보게 허락하시면 안 될 텐데.</u>

1 ⓐ와 같은 의미가 되도록 빈칸을 채워 문장을 완성하시오.

   → I am _____ tired _____ I _____ study now.

2 ⓑ의 우리말과 같은 뜻이 되도록 빈칸을 채워 문장을 완성하시오.

   → Your parents shouldn't _____ too much TV. (allow, watch)

A 다음 〈보기〉에서 알맞은 것을 골라 현재분사나 과거분사로 바꿔 문장을 완성하시오.

> 보기   fall   burn   bark   miss

1 경찰은 그 실종된 아이를 찾지 못했다.

→ The police couldn't find the _____ child.

2 짖는 개는 좀처럼 물지 않는다.

→ _____ dogs seldom bite.

3 많은 사람들은 낙엽을 밟고 걷는 것을 좋아한다.

→ Many people like walking on the _____ leaves.

4 그 소방관들은 불에 탄 목재의 잿더미를 보고 있었다.

→ The firefighters were looking at the ashes of _____ wood.

B 다음 두 문장이 같은 뜻이 되도록 빈칸에 알맞은 말을 쓰시오.

1 The villagers danced, as they sang loudly.

→ The villagers danced, _____ loudly .

2 This is a story. My English teacher wrote it.

→ This is a story _____ by my English teacher.

3 I have a friend. She lives in France.

→ I have a friend _____ in France.

C 다음 대화문을 읽고 물음에 답하시오.

Anna: Hi, Brian. You came back. How was your trip?

Brian: It was really ⓐ_____(excite), but I'm a bit ⓑ_____(tire) now.

Anna: Did you take many pictures?

Brian: No. I couldn't take pictures. When I opened my suitcase at the hotel,
(a) <u>나는 내 카메라가 부서져 있는 것을 발견했어.</u> (find, break).

Anna: That's too bad. Next time when you travel, make sure that you carry your
camera safely.

1 빈칸 ⓐ와 ⓑ에 주어진 단어의 알맞은 형태를 쓰시오.

ⓐ _____   ⓑ _____

2 (a)에 주어진 단어를 이용하여 우리말에 맞게 영작하시오.

→ _____ _____ _____ _____ _____.

A 다음 문장의 의미가 통하도록 분사구문을 이용하여 문장을 완성하시오.

1 The couple watched the movie and ate popcorn.

→ The couple watched the movie, _____.

2 After I graduated from high school, I could apply for a driver's license.

→ _____, I could apply for a driver's license.

3 Even though he is very tall, he always tries to sleep more than 8 hours.

→ _____, he always tries to sleep more than 8 hours.

4 Since they are different from other birds, penguins can't fly.

→ _____, penguins can't fly.

B 다음 〈보기〉에서 알맞은 접속사를 골라 두 문장이 같은 의미가 되도록 부사절을 완성하시오.

보기   if   because   while   although

1 Coming to the party, you'll see many movie stars.

→ _____, you'll see many movie stars.

2 Singing the song, she danced beautifully.

→ _____, she danced beautifully.

3 Feeling cold, the boy drank a glass of warm milk.

→ _____, the boy drank a glass of warm milk.

4 Not finishing his homework, he still wanted to play with his friends.

→ _____, he still wanted to play with his friends.

C 다음 우리말과 같은 뜻이 되도록 괄호 안의 단어를 알맞게 배열하여 분사로 시작하는 문장을 완성하시오.

1 그는 자신의 코트를 벗으면서 집에 들어갔다. (his coat, he, the house, taking off, entered)

→ _____

2 그는 패션에 관심이 있어서 그 학생은 이탈리아에 공부를 하러 갔다. (the student, fashion, to study, interested in, being, went to Italy)

→ _____

3 호숫가를 걷다가 나는 오리 가족을 보았다. (I, the lake, a duck family, saw, along, walking)

→ _____

4 화가 나서 그녀는 남동생에게 소리를 질렀다. (her little brother, she, angry, feeling, shouted at)

→ _____

A 다음 두 문장의 의미가 같도록 빈칸을 채우시오.

1 Because it is very cold outside, you'd better stay home today.

→ _____ very cold outside, you'd better stay home today.

2 When they are seen from above, the buildings look very small.

→ _____ from above, the buildings look very small.

3 The holiday being around the corner, everyone feels happy these days.

→ Since _____ around the corner, everyone feels happy these days.

4 Born and raised in Brazil, he can play soccer really well.

→ Because _____ in Brazil, he can play soccer really well.

B 다음 주어진 단어를 이용하여 우리말과 같은 뜻이 되도록 문장을 완성하시오.

1 너의 반응으로 판단하건대, 너는 내가 무슨 말하는지 모르는구나. (judge)

_____ your reaction, you have no idea what I am talking about.

2 Joe 얘기가 나와서 말인데, 파티에 그를 초대할거야? (speak)

_____ Joe, are you going to invite him to the party?

3 일반적으로 말하자면, 한국인은 매운 음식을 좋아해. (general)

_____, Koreans love spicy food.

4 솔직히 말해서, 너의 과자 중 하나를 먹었어. (frank)

_____, I ate one of your cookies.

C 다음 우리말과 같은 뜻이 되도록 주어진 단어를 알맞게 배열하시오.

1 우리는 점심을 많이 먹었음에도 아직도 배가 고프다. (a big lunch, we, are, had, still hungry, having)

→ _____

2 나는 전에 그녀를 만난 적이 있어서 그녀와 있을 때 편안했다. (having, her, her, around, before, felt comfortable, I, met)

→ _____

3 나는 지갑을 잃어버려서 버스를 탈 수 없다. (can't, lost, my wallet, the bus, I, having, take)

→ _____

4 그들은 중국에서 공부를 해서 중국어를 꽤 잘할 수 있다. (they, pretty well, in China, Chinese, speak, having, can, studied)

→ _____

A 다음 밑줄 친 부분을 가장 적절한 시제로 고쳐 쓰시오.

1 They <u>never try</u> Korean food until now. → _____

2 I <u>have seen</u> him at the library yesterday. → _____

3 We <u>have graduated</u> from elementary school 3 years ago. → _____

4 Hannah <u>has lost</u> her umbrella the day before yesterday. → _____

5 My parents <u>don't talk</u> to each other since last night. → _____

6 He <u>is playing</u> the video game since this morning. It must be really fun. → _____

B 다음 우리말과 같은 뜻이 되도록 주어진 동사를 이용하여 문장을 완성하시오.

1 그녀는 2016년 이후로 저 집에 살고 있다. (live, 2016)

→ She _____ in that house _____.

2 경찰은 3일 동안 그 아이를 찾는 중이다. (search, three)

→ The police _____ for the kid _____.

3 그 학생들은 지금까지 이 반에서 많은 문제를 겪어 왔다. (have)

→ The students _____ many problems in this class so far.

4 그 개는 이미 그 뼈다귀를 정원에 숨겼다. (hide, already)

→ The dog _____ the bone in the garden.

C 다음 대화문을 읽고 물음에 답하시오.

Mason: Hey, Hailey. I ⓐ <u>didn't expect</u> to see you here.

Hailey: Mason, what a nice surprise! What ⓑ <u>are you doing</u> here at the airport?

Mason: Well, I ⓒ <u>decided to take</u> my vacation. I'm off to Australia this afternoon.

Hailey: That's great. (a) 전에 호주에 가본 적이 있니? (Australia, before)

Mason: No, I haven't. I ⓓ <u>have been</u> to New Zealand three years ago, but this will be
my first time to Australia. I'm really looking forward to it.

Hailey: I ⓔ <u>have been</u> to Australia twice. I really like the outback.

1 (a)에 주어진 단어를 이용하여 우리말에 맞도록 영작하시오.

→ _____

2 ⓐ~ⓔ 중 어법상 바르지 않은 것을 찾아 고치시오.

_____ → _____

A 다음 문장의 밑줄 친 부분을 바르게 고치시오.

1 I had been going through a lot of stress at home lately. → _____

2 Sarah has already gone to the market when I called her. → _____

3 Melanie had been learning Russian since she moved to Russia. → _____

4 My uncle has worked at the hospital before he became an actor. → _____

5 Tim has been watching TV until the school bus came. → _____

B 다음 〈보기〉에서 두 문장의 의미가 통하도록 과거완료 또는 과거완료 진행형을 써서 문장을 완성하시오.

1 The customer paid for the potato chips, but she forgot to get her change.

→ The customer realized that she _____ to get her change.

2 My friend called me after I started doing my homework.

→ I _____ my homework when my friend called me.

3 The robot just cleaned the house, and a moment later, my parents came home.

→ When my parents came home, the robot _____ just _____ the house.

4 He was reading a novel, and a moment later, he heard a scream.

→ He _____ a novel when he heard a scream.

C 다음 우리말과 같은 뜻이 되도록 주어진 단어를 배열하시오.

1 그 예술가는 네 시간 동안 그림을 그리고 있었기 때문에 매우 피곤했다.

(been, four hours, had, for, painting, the artist)

→ _____, so she was exhausted.

2 어제 그 소년은 학교에 지각했다. 그 전에 그는 지각을 해본 적이 없었다.

(been, had, he, never, late)

→ Yesterday the boy was late for school. Before that, _____.

3 나는 댄스동아리에 들기 전에 그를 본 적이 없었다.

(him, seen, had, never, I)

→ _____ before I joined the dance club.

4 전화벨이 1분 동안 계속 울리고 있었지만, 아무도 집에 없었다.

(ringing, been, for a minute, had, the phone)

→ _____, but no one was at home.

A 다음 괄호 안에 주어진 말을 이용하여 빈칸에 알맞은 말을 쓰시오.

1 What language _____ in Argentina? (speak)

2 A new hospital _____ in town now. (build)

3 I am sure the TV show will _____ by many viewers. (love)

4 This letter _____ and sent by the president himself. (write)

5 All the passengers _____ to the hospital after the accident. (take)

B 다음 우리말과 같은 뜻이 되도록 보기에 있는 단어를 이용하여 문장을 완성하시오.

보기   include   change   unlock   delay

1 그들의 이름은 대기자 명단에 포함되어 있습니다.

→ Their names _____ _____ on the waiting list.

2 내가 문을 열려고 했을 때 나는 그것이 잠겨 있지 않음을 알았다.

→ When I tried to open the door, I found that it _____ _____.

3 짙은 안개로 인해 비행이 지연될 것입니다.

→ The flight _____ _____ _____ due to thick fog.

4 그 스케줄은 필요 시 변경될 수 있습니다.

→ The schedule _____ _____ _____ if necessary.

C 다음 우리말과 같은 뜻이 되도록 주어진 단어를 배열하시오.

1 그 학생은 드론 조종사로 고용되었다. (a drone pilot, hired, has, as, been)

→ The student _____.

2 그 새끼고양이는 나무에서 발견되었다. (in, found, was, the tree)

→ The kitten _____.

3 그 노트북 컴퓨터는 나의 형에 의해 수리되고 있었다. (being, my brother, was, by, repaired)

→ The laptop computer _____.

4 당신의 세탁기는 일주일 안으로 배달될 것입니다. (a week, delivered, within, be, will)

→ Your washing machine _____.

A 다음 〈보기〉에서 알맞은 단어를 골라 문장을 완성하시오.

> 보기   for   to   of

1 This apple pie was cooked _____ us by my aunt.

2 An unknown package was sent _____ the police officer.

3 Some personal questions were asked _____ him by the interviewer.

B 다음 문장을 간접목적어와 직접목적어를 주어로 한 수동태 문장으로 바꿔 쓰시오.

1 Mr. Barnes taught us African history.

→ _____

→ _____

2 I paid him ten dollars for the damage.

→ _____

→ _____

3 Daniel gave Emily a piece of advice.

→ _____

→ _____

4 Some students ask him silly questions during class.

→ _____

→ _____

C 다음 우리말과 같은 뜻이 되도록 주어진 단어를 활용하여 수동태 문장을 완성하시오.

1 사슴 한 마리가 길을 건너는 모습이 목격되었다. (see, cross)

→ A deer _____ the street.

2 나는 조용히 해달라고 요구 받았다. (ask, keep it down)

→ I _____ .

3 그 소녀들은 체육관에서 배드민턴을 하는 것이 발견되었다. (find, play)

→ The girls _____ badminton in the gym.

4 학생들은 부모님께 편지를 써야 했다. (make, write)

→ The students _____ letters to their parents.

A 다음 〈보기〉에서 알맞은 단어를 골라 문장을 완성하시오. (중복 불가)

> 보기   in   of   to   with

1 This table is made _____ glass.

2 My car was covered _____ snow.

3 Now her secrets are known _____ all of her neighbors.

4 Your brother is interested _____ buying a new bike.

B 다음 우리말과 같은 뜻이 되도록 주어진 단어를 배열하시오.

1 그녀의 아이디어는 반에 있는 모든 사람들에게 비웃음을 당했다. (by everyone, laughed, in the class, at, her ideas, were)

→ _____

2 그 운 좋은 개는 그 택시에 의해 치이지 않았다. (wasn't, the lucky dog, by the taxi, over, run)

→ _____

3 그 아이들은 보모에 의해 돌봐질 거야. (by a babysitter, be, care, will, the children, taken, of)

→ _____

4 그 계획은 곧장 실행되어야 합니다. (should, right away, out, be, the plan, carried)

→ _____

C 다음 대화문을 읽고 물음에 답하시오.

A: Hey, how was your trip?

B: It was great. ⓐ It was my first school trip. ⓑ Every time the trip called off because of bad weather, I was very disappointed.

A: ⓒ I can imagine how excited you were this time! Where did you go?

B: We went to the Independence Hall of Korea. ⓓ I was shocked at what happened in Korea under Japanese rule. I think that ⓔ the tragic history of Korea should be known to all teenagers, and (a) we should look up to the fighters for national independence. Have you ever been there?

A: Never, but I hope I can visit it someday.

1 ⓐ~ⓔ 중 어법상 바르지 않은 것을 찾아 바르게 고치시오.

_____ → _____

2 (a)를 수동태 문장으로 바꿔 쓰시오.

→ _____

A 다음 〈보기〉에서 알맞은 것을 골라 문장을 완성하시오. (중복 가능)

> **보기** got used to   may well   cannot

1 그 외국인들은 마침내 김치 먹는 것에 익숙해졌다.

→ The foreigners finally _____ eating kimchi.

2 해커로부터 컴퓨터를 보호할 때는 아무리 신중해도 지나치지 않다.

→ You _____ be too serious when protecting your computer from hackers.

3 나는 그녀의 제안을 따를 수밖에 없다.

→ I _____ but listen to her suggestion.

4 너는 그가 약간 이상하다고 생각하는 것은 당연하다.

→ You _____ think he is a bit strange.

B 다음 문장에서 밑줄 친 부분을 바르게 고치시오.

1 There <u>would</u> be a bakery in front of the bank.

2 This machine is used to <u>drilling</u> holes in the wall.

3 You <u>may as well as</u> ask for help right now.

4 We <u>can</u> be too careful when treating patients.

C 다음 대화문을 읽고 물음에 답하시오.

A: Dad, what did you use to do for fun when you were young?

B: Well, I ⓐ_____ go swimming and fishing in the river.

A: And what about wintertime?

B: I went skating on the frozen river.

A: It sounds dangerous.

B: Yeah, but I (a) <u>could not but</u> playing on the ice. It was so fun.

A: I want to try that some time.

B: We ⓑ_____ hope this winter is really cold for ice skating.

1 주어진 단어를 이용하여 ⓐ와 ⓑ를 알맞게 채우시오.

ⓐ _____ (use)

ⓑ _____ (might)

2 (a)의 틀린 부분을 바르게 고치시오.

→ _____

A 다음 우리말에 알맞게 빈칸에 알맞은 조동사를 쓰시오.

1 그녀는 불을 끄지 않은 것이 틀림없다.

→ She _____ not have turned off the light.

2 그 축구선수는 골을 넣을 수 있었는데.

→ The soccer player _____ have scored.

3 그 학생은 내가 말한 것을 들었을지도 몰라.

→ The student _____ have heard what I said.

4 그들은 그들의 숙제를 했어야 했는데.

→ They _____ have done their homework.

5 Richard가 그 스포츠카를 샀었을 리가 없다.

→ Richard _____ have bought the sports car.

B 다음 〈보기〉에서 알맞은 말을 골라 문장을 완성하시오.

> 보기　　must have　　could have　　cannot have　　shouldn't have

1 You _____ put the syrup in it. It's too sweet.

2 He didn't log in. He _____ forgotten the password.

3 Why didn't you ask for help? I _____ given you some good ideas.

4 The room was so quiet. She _____ been in the room.

C 다음 짝지어진 두 문장이 같은 뜻이 되도록 주어진 단어와 「조동사 + have + p.p.」 구문을 사용하여 문장을 완성하시오.

1 You had to take the pills, but you didn't.

→ You _____. (should)

2 I'm sure that the student cheated on the test.

→ The student _____. (must)

3 I'm sure that she didn't see me last night. I stayed home all day long yesterday.

→ She _____. (cannot)

4 It is possible that he ran into the movie star at the mall.

→ He _____. (might)

A 다음 우리말에 맞게 빈칸을 채워 문장을 완성하시오.

1 돌고래는 심지어 개보다 더 똑똑하다. (even, intelligent)

→ Dolphins are _____ than dogs.

2 그 놀이공원은 우리가 예측한 것보다 훨씬 더 붐볐다. (much, crowded)

→ The amusement park was _____ than we expected.

3 그녀의 건강 상태는 간호사가 우리에게 설명한 것보다 더 안 좋았다. (far, bad)

→ Her medical conditions were _____ than the nurse explained to us.

B 다음 두 문장의 의미가 같도록 빈칸을 채우시오.

1 As he made more money, he felt less happy.

→ _____ money he made, _____ he felt.

2 My boss was rich, and she has made much more money this year.

→ My boss got _____ and _____.

3 As the product becomes more expensive, more people want to buy it.

→ _____ the product becomes, _____ people want to buy it.

4 The price of this machine is higher than the price of your car.

→ The price of this machine is higher than _____ of your car.

C 다음 대화문을 읽고 물음에 답하시오.

A: I heard you got a train ticket for the holidays. I envy you. I tried to log onto the train
website, but it seemed that everyone was ⓐ [faster than / as fast as] I was.
The tickets were sold out. I'm going to drive this time. It'll be far slower than taking
the train because of heavy traffic.

B: Yeah, but at least you can leave whenever you want, and I think it's much
ⓑ [comfortable / more comfortable] than taking the train. I prefer a car ⓒ [than / to]
a train, but I don't have a car.

A: But I hate to be stuck in traffic, so I'll leave home as early as I can. (a) 내가 일찍 떠나면
떠날수록 교통 체증은 덜 할 거야.

1 ⓐ~ⓒ의 괄호 안에서 알맞은 것을 고르시오.

ⓐ _____ ⓑ _____ ⓒ _____

2 괄호 안에 주어진 단어를 이용하여 (a)의 우리말에 맞도록 문장을 완성하시오.

→ _____ (early) I leave, _____ (little) traffic there will be.

A 다음 〈보기〉에서 알맞은 것을 골라 as ~ as를 사용하여 문장을 완성하시오.

> 보기   slowly   soon   great   long   messy   quickly

1 The police officer ran _____ he could to catch the robber.

2 You'd better call me _____ you get home.

3 Please speak _____ possible so I can understand you.

4 You can stay here _____ you want.

5 There is no basketball player _____ Michael Jordan.

6 Your bedroom is not _____ mine.

B 다음 주어진 문장과 의미가 통하도록 문장을 완성하시오.

1 Chris is not as thoughtful as Jake.

→ Chris _____ Jake.

→ Jake _____ Chris.

2 Your cat is not as fluffy as mine.

→ Your cat _____ mine.

→ My cat _____ yours.

C 다음 주어진 단어를 이용하여 문장을 완성하시오.

1 의사는 그에게 가능한 한 적게 먹으라고 말했다. (little)

→ The doctor told him to eat _____.

2 너의 집은 그녀의 집보다 방의 수가 2배이다. (as, many, hers)

→ Your house has _____.

3 Kelly는 언니보다 세 배나 더 많이 운동했다. (as, much)

→ Kelly exercised _____.

4 그 가수들은 가능한 한 크게 노래할 것이다. (loudly, can)

→ The singers will sing _____.

5 그의 연봉은 내 것보다 네 배나 많다. (time, great, than)

→ His salary is _____.

A 다음 우리말과 같은 뜻이 되도록 괄호 안의 단어를 사용하여 문장을 완성하시오.

1 그녀는 세계에서 가장 유명한 여배우 중 한 명이다. (famous, actress)

→ She is _____ in the world.

2 대구는 한국에서 가장 더운 도시 중 하나이다. (hot, city)

→ Daegu is _____ in Korea.

3 Emma는 내가 알고 있던 사람 중에서 가장 놀라운 사람이다. (amazing, ever, know)

→ Emma is _____ that _____.

4 이것은 내가 본 영화 중에서 가장 지루한 영화이다. (boring, ever, watch)

→ This is _____ that _____.

B 다음 우리말과 같은 뜻이 되도록 주어진 단어를 배열하시오.

1 나의 아기는 다른 어떤 악기 소리보다 피아노 소리를 좋아한다. (musical instrument's, than, better, any other)

→ My baby likes the sound of the piano _____.

2 네 자신을 믿는 것보다 중요한 것은 없다. (believing in, nothing, as important as, yourself, is)

→ _____.

3 이것은 내가 운전해 본 차 중 가장 빠른 차다. (driven, is, the fastest car, ever, that, this, I've)

→ _____.

C 다음 문장을 〈보기〉와 같이 바꿔 쓰시오.

> 보기 Sophia is the tallest student in the class.
>
> → No (other) student in the class is taller than Sophia.
> → No (other) student in the class is as tall as Sophia.
> → Sophia is taller than any other student in the class.

1 That is the cheapest product in the shop.

→ _____

→ _____

→ _____

2 Mike was the most friendly person in the neighborhood.

→ _____

→ _____

→ _____

A 다음 주어진 단어를 이용하여 가정법 문장을 완성하시오.

1 If I _____ you, I would ask for help. (be)

2 If he _____ an only child, he would be very lonely. (be)

3 If you _____ a car, you wouldn't have to take the bus. (have)

4 If she cooked regularly, her food _____ taste better. (will)

5 If the band sang better, they _____ become more popular. (can)

B 다음 우리말과 같은 뜻이 되도록 주어진 단어를 이용하여 문장을 완성하시오.

1 오늘이 너의 생일이라면, 너는 선물을 많이 받을 텐데. (be, will, get)

→ If today _____ your birthday, you _____ many presents.

2 걱정하지 마. 우리가 좀 더 노력하면, 한 골 더 넣을 거야. (try, will, score)

→ Don't worry. If we _____ harder, we _____ another goal.

3 내가 스페인에서 태어났더라면, 스페인어를 잘할 수 있을 텐데. (be, can, speak)

→ If I _____ born in Spain, I _____ Spanish well.

4 그가 숙제를 했더라면, 그의 어머니께서 화나지 않으셨을 텐데. (do, will, be, angry)

→ If he _____ his homework, his mother _____ angry.

C 다음 두 문장의 의미가 통하도록 가정법 문장을 완성하시오.

1 As he doesn't have enough money, he can't travel around Europe.

→ _____

2 As Keith and I don't go to the same school, we don't see each other often.

→ _____

3 As she has gained weight, this dress doesn't fit her now.

→ _____

4 As I didn't have breakfast, I am hungry now.

→ _____

A 다음 우리말과 같은 뜻이 되도록 주어진 단어를 이용하여 가정법 문장을 완성하시오.

1 그가 그 말을 하지 않았었더라면 좋았을 텐데. (wish, say)

→ I _____ that.

2 그녀는 마치 슬픈 것처럼 보인다. (사실은 슬프지 않다.) (as if, be)

→ She looks _____ sad.

3 그는 마치 대통령을 직접 만났던 것처럼 말한다. (사실은 만나지 않았다) (as if, meet)

→ He talks _____ the president himself.

B 다음 〈보기〉와 같이 문장을 바꿔 쓰시오.

> **보기**   Without your help, they couldn't solve this problem.
>
> → <u>If it were not for your help</u>, they couldn't solve this problem.
>
> → <u>But for your help</u>, they couldn't solve this problem.

1 Without the Internet, it wouldn't be easy to collect data.

→ _____, it wouldn't be easy to collect data.

→ _____, it wouldn't be easy to collect data.

2 But for the map, we would have gotten lost in the woods.

→ _____, we would have gotten lost in the woods.

→ _____, we would have gotten lost in the woods.

C 다음 대화문을 읽고 물음에 답하시오.

Ryan: Hi, Henry. Have you decided which club to join? If you ⓐ <u>are</u> interested in K-pop music, you can join our music club.

Henry: I really like ⓑ <u>listening</u> to K-pop music, but I already ⓒ <u>joined</u> the movie club. If you had asked me earlier, I ⓓ <u>would join</u> your club. Can we participate in more than one club activity?

Ryan: I'm afraid, we ⓔ <u>can't</u>. It's a school policy; one club activity only. (a) <u>우리가 원하는 만큼 많은 클럽에 참여할 수 있으면 좋을 텐데.</u>

Henry: Yeah, I totally agree with you.

1 ⓐ~ⓔ 중 어법상 바르지 않은 것을 알맞게 고치시오.

_____ → _____

2 괄호 안에 주어진 단어를 이용하여 (a)의 우리말에 맞도록 문장을 완성하시오.

→ _____ (can, take part in) as many club activities as we want.

A 다음 빈칸에 알맞은 관계대명사를 넣어 문장을 완성하시오.

1 I have a French friend _____ name is Julien.

2 The actor _____ he knows is my brother.

3 The dish _____ she made for dinner was tasty.

4 The book _____ you're reading is very interesting.

5 That's the teacher _____ I like most in my school.

B 다음 두 문장을 관계대명사로 연결할 때 빈칸에 알맞은 말을 쓰시오

1 The waiter was very kind. He was serving us.

→ The waiter _____ was very kind.

2 The bus runs every half hour. It goes to Lake Park.

→ The bus _____ runs every half hour.

3 Mary is the girl. I want to invite her.

→ Mary is the girl _____.

4 My grandmother often bakes cookies. The cookies have a lot of nuts.

→ My grandmother often bakes cookies _____.

5 Sam was an architect. He designed many buildings.

→ Sam was an architect _____.

6 Look at the house. Its walls are painted in yellow.

→ Look at the house _____.

C 다음 대화문을 읽고 ⓐ∼ⓒ에 들어갈 알맞은 말을 〈보기〉에서 골라 넣으시오.

Daniel: Do you know someone ⓐ_____ is in the music business?

Julie: Yes. My brother is a songwriter.

Daniel: That's great. I need to interview a person ⓑ_____ job is related to music. Can I interview him?

Julie: Yes. Do you want to do that now? He is working in the studio ⓒ_____ is only 5 minutes away from here.

Daniel: Yes. Thank you so much.

| 보기 | which | who | whose |

ⓐ _____   ⓑ _____   ⓒ _____

A 다음 빈칸에 what과 that 중 알맞은 것을 써넣으시오.

1 That's not _____ I meant to say.

2 Nobody knows _____ will happen next.

3 This is the same bag _____ I lost last Friday.

4 Please tell me _____ you want for your birthday.

5 Show me the camera _____ you bought yesterday.

B 다음 우리말과 같은 뜻이 되도록 주어진 단어를 알맞게 배열하시오.

1 우리가 마실 것이 있나요? (can, we, that, drink)

→ Is there anything _____ ?

2 그가 한 말은 그녀를 화나게 만들었다. (said, he, what)

→ _____ made her angry.

3 Allison은 내가 가진 우산과 똑같은 것을 가지고 있다. (have, that, I)

→ Allison has the same umbrella _____ .

4 나는 네가 지난밤에 한 일을 알고 있다. (you, what, last, did, night)

→ I know _____ .

5 내가 정말로 하고 싶은 것은 그저 잠을 자는 것이다. (what, do, I, to, want, really)

→ _____ is just sleep.

C 다음 글을 읽고 물음에 답하시오.

When you eat or write, which hand do you use, right hand or left hand? A person who
ⓐ_____ (use) the left hand for everyday things is left-handed. Two to three of ten
people use their left hand for writing or eating. They have difficulty when they try to
use objects that ⓑ_____ (be) made for right-handed people. Left-handed people who
ⓒ_____ (have) experienced many difficulties created a special day. It is called "Left-
handers Day." On this day, right-handed people can experience how hard the left-
handed people live. But (a) 왼손잡이들이 진정으로 원하는 것은 동정심이 아니다. (want, left-handed
people, sympathy, not, what, is, really)

1 ⓐ~ⓒ에 주어진 단어의 알맞은 형태를 쓰시오.

ⓐ _____   ⓑ _____   ⓒ _____

2 (a)의 우리말과 같은 뜻이 되도록 주어진 단어를 알맞게 배열하시오.

→ _____

A 다음 빈칸에 알맞은 관계부사를 써넣으시오.

1 I forgot the place _____ I put my smartphone.

2 The hotel _____ we stayed was clean and quiet.

3 I always remember the day _____ I first met you.

4 The reason _____ I called you is to tell you something important.

5 Everyone wanted to know _____ I could arrive there on time.

6 Please tell me the exact time _____ you can meet me.

B 다음 두 문장을 관계부사를 사용하여 한 문장으로 만드시오. (단, 관계부사와 선행사 생략 금지)

1 This is the village. My friend lives here.

→ _____

2 We went to the city. My grandparents used to live there.

→ _____

3 This is the hospital. My father works here as a surgeon.

→ _____

4 March 15th is the day. My little sister was born on this day.

→ _____

C 다음 우리말과 같은 뜻이 되도록 주어진 단어를 이용하여 문장을 완성하시오.

1 네가 여기에 언제 도착했는지 알고 싶어. (arrive)

→ I'd like to know the time at _____.

2 네가 내 컴퓨터를 어떻게 고쳤는지 말해 줄래? (way, fix)

→ Can you tell me _____?

3 너는 그가 왜 마음을 바꿨는지 이유를 아니? (change)

→ Do you know the reason for _____?

4 이곳이 나의 작품이 전시되어 있는 미술관이다. (exhibit)

→ This is the art museum in _____.

A 다음 짝지어진 두 문장이 같은 뜻이 되도록 빈칸에 알맞은 복합관계대명사를 써넣으시오.

1 I will buy you anything that you want.

→ I will buy you _____ you want.

2 Anyone who comes first will be first served.

→ _____ comes first will be first served.

3 No matter what happens, I'll believe you.

→ _____ happens, I'll believe you.

4 No matter which you choose, you will be disappointed.

→ _____ you choose, you will be disappointed.

B 다음 우리말과 같은 뜻이 되도록 빈칸에 알맞은 복합관계부사를 써넣으시오.

1 당신이 무엇을 하든 나는 당신과 함께할 거예요.

→ _____ you do, I'll be with you.

2 네가 편할 때 아무 때나 우리 집에 놀러 와.

→ Come to my place _____ it is convenient for you.

3 그 어리석은 남자는 자신이 원하는 사람과 누구든지 결혼할 수 있다고 믿는다.

→ The foolish man believes that he can marry _____ he wants.

4 우리는 당신이 가길 원하는 곳은 어디든지 데려다 줄 것이다.

→ We will take you _____ you want to go.

5 아무리 노력을 한다 해도 너는 내일까지 그 일을 마무리하지 못할 것이다.

→ _____ hard you try, you can't finish the work by tomorrow.

C 다음 우리말과 같은 뜻이 되도록 주어진 단어와 복합관계사를 사용하여 문장을 완성하시오.

1 너는 무엇을 사더라도 만족하지 못할 것이다. (buy)

→ _____, you won't be satisfied.

2 그녀가 어디를 가든지 그녀의 개는 그녀를 따라다닌다. (go)

→ _____, her dog follows her.

3 그 노래를 들을 때마다 할머니 생각이 난다. (listen to)

→ _____, it reminds me of my grandmother.

4 나는 그들이 무슨 말을 하더라도 나의 꿈을 포기하지 않을 것이다. (say)

→ _____, I'll never give up my dream.

A 다음 빈칸에 whether와 that 중 알맞은 것을 써넣으시오.

1 He told me _____ I should accept their apology.

2 I want to know _____ the traffic is heavy or not.

3 I'm not sure _____ I can get there on time or not.

4 It is uncertain _____ Korea will win the match or not.

5 The rumor _____ she was a model surprised us.

B 다음 문장을 〈보기〉와 같이 바꿔 쓰시오.

> 보기 That he passed the exam was lucky.
>
> → It was lucky that he passed the exam.

1 That Sandra told me a lie is clear.

→ _____

2 That he had a car accident is sad.

→ _____

3 That we met again in another city was fate.

→ _____

4 That you are suffering from many allergies is a big problem.

→ _____

C 다음 우리말과 같은 뜻이 되도록 괄호 안의 단어를 이용하여 문장을 완성하시오.

1 그는 자신이 선글라스를 쓰고 있는 것을 알아차리지 못했다. (wear, sunglasses)

→ He didn't notice _____.

2 나는 그가 아직도 그 책을 읽고 싶어 하는지 궁금하다. (still, want)

→ I'm wondering _____.

3 Chris가 회사를 그만 둘 거라는 소문은 거짓으로 드러났다. (will, leave the company)

→ The rumor _____ turned out to be false.

4 우리 차를 팔지 말지를 결정하는 것은 우리에게 너무 어려운 일이다. (will, sell, not)

→ It is too difficult to decide _____.

A 다음 문장에서 어법상 어색한 부분을 찾아 바르게 고치시오.

1 Do you think which is cheaper?

    _____ → _____

2 Can you tell me why is he happy?

    _____ → _____

3 I wonder that whether my answer is right.

    _____ → _____

4 I have no idea how does she feel about Jason.

    _____ → _____

B 다음 두 문장을 한 문장으로 바꾸시오.

1 Can you tell me? + Who do you like most?

    → _____

2 Do you know? + Where is the treasure buried?

    → _____

3 Does she know? + What does he want for his birthday gift?

    → _____

4 I wonder. + Does she work for a bank?

    → _____

5 Do you believe? + When did they leave home?

    → _____

C 다음 우리말과 같은 뜻이 되도록 주어진 말을 알맞게 배열하여 문장을 완성하시오.

1 우리는 그의 이름을 모른다. (his name, what, we, don't, know, is)

    → _____

2 나는 그녀가 학생인지 아닌지 궁금하다. (wonder, I, whether, a student, she, is, or not)

    → _____

3 너는 그가 언제 공항에 도착하는지 아니? (do, arrives, you, when, know, he, at the airport)

    → _____

4 그녀는 어제 그 영화를 봤는지 내게 물었다. (I, watched, yesterday, she, the movie, asked, me, whether)

    → _____

A 다음 〈보기〉에서 알맞은 것을 골라 문장을 완성하시오.

> 보기   if   unless   and   or

1   Put on a coat, _____ you will catch a cold.

2   _____ you help me, I can finish this on time.

3   _____ I get a job soon, I'll be in trouble.

4   Turn left at the corner, _____ you will see the bank.

B 다음 우리말과 같은 뜻이 되도록 문장을 완성하시오.

1   내가 집에 도착하면 전화할게.

    → I will call you _____ I get home.

2   내가 없는 동안 전화 좀 받아줄래?

    → Can you answer the phone _____ I am away?

3   영화가 시작할 때까지 15분이 남았다.

    → We have 15 minutes _____ the movie starts.

4   밖에 나가기 전에 모든 문이 잠겼는지 확인해라.

    → Make sure all the doors are locked _____ you go out.

C 다음 대화문을 읽고 물음에 답하시오.

Amy:	What were you doing when I called you last night?
Brandon:	Oh, I'm sorry. (a) <u>네가 전화했을 때 자고 있었어.</u> (me, called, you, was sleeping, when, I) By the way, why did you call me?
Amy:	I have two movie tickets for tonight. I wonder ⓐ_____ you want to see it with me.
Brandon:	Sure. I think that it will be the first time we go to the movies together.
Amy:	Right. We haven't seen a movie together since we met.
Brandon:	Let's meet in front of your house. The theater is not far from your house, so we can walk ⓑ_____ it doesn't rain.
Amy:	That sounds great. Since you have tickets, I'll buy popcorn. See you.

1   (a)에 주어진 단어를 우리말에 맞도록 알맞게 배열하여 문장을 완성하시오.

    → _____

2   빈칸 ⓐ와 ⓑ에 공통으로 들어갈 접속사를 쓰시오.

    → _____

A 다음 〈보기〉에서 알맞은 것을 골라 문장을 완성하시오.

> **보기**   because   because of   even though   in spite of

1 He can't go to school _____ a bad cold.

2 She is hungry _____ she skipped breakfast.

3 _____ all her efforts, she couldn't pass the exam.

4 _____ I called her name loudly, she didn't hear me.

B 다음 우리말과 같은 뜻이 되도록 문장을 완성하시오.

1 봄이지만 아직도 춥다.

→ _____ it is spring, it is still cold.

2 그는 가난할지라도 매우 행복하다.

→ He is very happy _____ his poverty.

3 소음 때문에 나는 운전에 집중할 수 없었다.

→ I couldn't concentrate on driving _____ the noise.

4 나쁜 날씨에도 불구하고, 우리는 소풍을 갔다.

→ We went on a picnic _____ the bad weather.

5 마이크가 고장 났기 때문에, 연설가는 그의 목소리를 높여야 했다.

→ _____ the microphone was dead, the speaker had to raise his voice.

C 다음 글을 읽고 물음에 답하시오.

> My Russian husband, Yuri, and I have been living in the U.S.A. ⓐ since we got married.
> He and I usually communicate in English. ⓑ Although he thinks ⓒ that I should learn
> Russian, he doesn't think that he should learn Korean. Another problem is ⓓ that he has
> many Russian friends, and they speak Russian only. (a) _____ they come over, I'm left
> out ⓔ because of I can't speak Russian. The same situation happens (b) _____ we go
> to their house.

1 ⓐ~ⓔ 중 어법상 바르지 않은 것을 알맞게 고치시오.

_____ → _____

2 (a)와 (b)에 공통으로 들어갈 수 있는 접속사를 쓰시오.

→ _____

A 다음 문장을 간접화법 문장으로 바꿔 문장을 완성하시오.

1 Jack said, "I lost my wallet yesterday."

→ Jack said _____.

2 Grace said, "I will visit my grandmother this Saturday."

→ Grace said _____.

3 My teacher said to me, "You have to come here on time."

→ My teacher told me _____

4 Mom said, "You can eat ice cream after the meal."

→ Mom said _____.

B 다음 문장을 직접화법 문장으로 바꿔 문장을 완성하시오.

1 She told me that she would be a writer.

→ She said to me, "_____."

2 My mom said that it might rain that day.

→ My mom said, "_____."

3 The teacher told us not to make any noise.

→ The teacher said to us, "_____."

4 Brian said (that) his family would move to the urban area.

→ Brian said, "_____."

C 다음 글의 밑줄 친 문장을 간접화법 문장으로 바꿔 쓰시오.

My sister and I took the final tests two weeks ago. I was expecting good grades because I studied very hard for the test. Today we finally got our report cards. My sister made it to the top in her class, but I got poor grades. She said that she was praised by her teacher in front of her classmates. (a) My mother said to her, "I'm so proud of you." I was very depressed not because I didn't get good grades, but because I did study hard for the final test. My mother told me that it was okay because I did my best, and I could receive better grades next time. My sister also said she would help me study. Now I'm happy that I have a good sister who will help me study and a mother who understands me well.

→ My mother told her that _____.

A 다음 문장을 간접화법 문장으로 바꿔 문장을 완성하시오.

1 She said to me, "Why do you look so angry?"

→ She asked me _____.

2 The man said to me, "Where is the nearest subway station?"

→ The man asked me _____.

3 Jessica said to me, "What did you do with your brother yesterday?"

→ Jessica asked me _____.

B 다음 문장을 간접화법 문장으로 바꿔 문장을 완성하시오.

1 Ella said to me, "Can I borrow your pen?"

→ Ella asked me _____.

2 Lucy said to me, "Have you been to Brazil?"

→ Lucy asked me _____.

3 He said to me, "Do you know her phone number?"

→ He asked me _____.

4 Frank said to me, "Were you at the party yesterday?"

→ Frank asked me _____.

C 다음은 직접화법 문장을 간접화법 문장으로 전환한 것이다. 어법상 어색한 부분을 찾아 바르게 고치시오.

1 He said to me, "Do you like chocolate cake?"

→ He asked me that I liked chocolate cake.

_____ → _____

2 She said to me, "When will you come home tonight?"

→ She asked me whether when I would come home that night.

_____ → _____

3 Ben said to me, "Can you lend me some money?"

→ Ben asked me if he could lend him some money.

_____ → _____

4 Cathy said to him, "What are you going to do on Sunday?

→ Cathy asked him if he was going to do on Sunday.

_____ → _____

A 다음 밑줄 친 부분을 강조하는 문장으로 바꿔 쓰시오.

1 I understand my mom.

→ I _____

2 He tried his best to pass the exam.

→ He _____

3 I found my smartphone on the desk.

→ It was _____

4 Mark majored in accounting at the University of Oxford.

→ It was _____

5 I know little about Spanish.

→ _____

6 I've never seen such a beautiful sight.

→ _____

B 다음 대화에서 so나 neither를 이용하여 우리말에 맞게 답변을 완성하시오.

1 A: I am so happy now.

B: _____ (나도 그래.)

2 A: I don't enjoy watching horror movies.

B: _____ (나도 그래.)

C 다음 대화문의 밑줄 친 문장을 주어진 단어를 강조하는 문장으로 바꾸시오.

A: It's almost nine o'clock, and Jack hasn't come here yet. I wonder why he is so late.

B: I'm sorry that I didn't tell you. He told me he wouldn't come because he caught a cold.

A: Did you meet him?

B: No, but ⓐ he called me last night. He asked me to tell you he was really sorry for not coming. He will join us next time.

A: Jack must be very sick because ⓑ he hardly breaks his promises.

B: I know. We should be careful not to catch a cold.

ⓐ _____ (called)

ⓑ _____ (hardly)

A 다음 괄호 안에 주어진 동사를 이용하여 문장을 완성하시오.

1 I think that he _____ the news every day. (watch)

2 My brother said that he _____ a taxi yesterday. (take)

3 She knew that he _____ to be a doctor. (want)

4 I didn't understand why she _____ to Canada. (go)

5 I learned Galileo Galilei _____ telescopes. (developed)

6 She was very proud that her son _____ first prize in the competition. (win)

B 다음 괄호 안에 주어진 동사를 이용하여 현재시제의 문장을 완성하시오.

1 Both Sandy and I _____ to eat pizza. (want)

2 Either I or my sister _____ to babysit Tom. (need)

3 Not only you but also I _____ so busy that we cannot watch the movie. (be)

4 Physics _____ not a popular subject among undergraduates. (be)

5 A number of students suffering from a bad cold _____ absent today. (be)

6 A few dollars _____ a lot to the homeless. (mean)

C 다음 우리말과 일치하도록 괄호에 주어진 말을 이용하여 영작하시오.

1 그는 그녀가 반장이 될 거라고 생각했다. (the class president)

→ He thought that _____.

2 나는 한국전쟁이 1950년에 발발했다는 것을 안다. (the Korean War, break out)

→ I know that _____.

3 그 대학의 유학생 수는 10% 증가했다. (number, international, at the college, have grown)

→ _____ by 10%.

4 각 나라는 고유의 전통과 문화를 가지고 있다 (country, own, traditions, cultures)

→ _____